FAÇADE

lucia mia.   Bergoualla.   Che buona mi sa.

Contents

First published in this edition 1987
Gerald Duckworth & Co Ltd
The Old Piano Factory
43 Gloucester Crescent, London NW1

ISBN 0 7156 2184 X

British Library Cataloguing in Publication Data

Sitwell, Edith
  Façade
  I. Title   II. Hunter, Pamela
  821'.912   PR6037.18

  ISBN 0-7156-2184-X

Photoset in North Wales by
Derek Doyle & Associates, Mold, Clwyd
Printed in Great Britain by
Redwood Burn Limited, Trowbridge

Edith Sitwell

FAÇADE

with an interpretation by

Pamela Hunter

Duckworth

Preface

For too long *Façade*, the work for which Edith Sitwell is most widely recognized, has been applauded simply as a delightful concert entertainment featuring William Walton's music.

But what do the *poems* mean? It was this question that I asked myself, and the answers as I found them are presented in the following pages. For me Edith Sitwell's genius lay not only in the organization of words in rhythmical patterns accented appropriately to fit the music, but in her ability to cram a revelation into each poem, as a direct comment on her life and times. Just as the music of *Façade* has found its way alone into the concert hall with the First and Second Orchestral Suites (1926, 1938), and has been interpreted visually as a ballet since 1929, so the purpose of this book is to look at the poems in themselves.

It was while preparing to portray Edith Sitwell in a scenic production and BBC film of *Façade* that I became involved in the intricacies of her poetry. The first requirement of any actress is to understand the words to be communicated, and as I studied the poems and Edith Sitwell's biography the link between the two became clear. It was fascinating to see how she was able to mask her thoughts behind the technical brilliance of the poems.

In order to present and interpret these thoughts I conceived the idea of writing short imaginary 'scenes' evoked in me by a reading of each poem and by what I knew of her life, to be followed by a brief explanatory commentary on each poem. I hope this book will do something to revive an interest in Edith Sitwell's poetry and lead at least to a fresh appraisal and understanding of *Façade*.

Over the years a total of 37 poems have appeared at various times under the title of *Façade*, beginning with only 9 published in 1922. This book contains the 21 poems which are performed with Walton's music and generally known today.

My warmest thanks must go to Francis and Susanna Sitwell for their encouragement and for the opportunity to meet Sacheverell Sitwell – the only remaining close link to Edith and her *Façade* – and also to Tony Palmer who, after seeing my performance in Zurich, told me to write this book.

May 1987   P.H.

Introduction

'Poetry cannot be entirely the work of the poet. It must be or should be, in part the conception of the reader.'

'In any case it is not the facts in a poem that make it interesting, but the effects on the mind of their observer.'

'Poetry is more like a crystal globe, with Truth imprisoned in it, like a fly in amber. The poet is the magician who fashions the crystal globe. But the reader is the magician who can find in these scintillating flaws, or translucent depths, some new undiscovered land.'

These words of Osbert Sitwell, written in 1921,[1] contain the justification for this book. The 'interpretation' of *Façade* that I offer here is simply an attempt to define the meanings of the poetry. By using a combination of invented scenes and a commentary, both biographical and analytical, I hope to be able to impart what *Façade* means to me, and what it might mean to the reader.

The most important point in dealing with Edith Sitwell's poetry is to accept her premise that 'the child's mind is reflected in the Artist's experience'.[2] The artist must retain the bright vision of childhood – the sensitivity to impressions and atmosphere, the intense fantastic seriousness. In the child's mind, 'life is a series of sharp outlines, bright flashing colours and strange meetings'.[3]

---

[1] Osbert Sitwell, *Who Killed Cock Robin?*, pp. 5-7.
[2] Edith Sitwell, *Children's Tales from the Russian Ballet Retold* (1920), p. 23.
[3] Ibid., p. 22.

9

'To a child, every person is a house in which the queerest people live – hiding behind strange doors, appearing only occasionally at darkened windows.'[4]

The adult has learnt to build his façade – his inner thoughts are well hidden. He is educated to 'understand' so that the world remains in his grasp – entirely material, mortal.

In Edith's poetry the imagination has free reign. Logic becomes that of a child – it may seem untruthful, images just appear – grow like the 'magic' of a flower out of the earth. The child is half seraph/half animal. For him the simple things hold wonder – fresh and unjaded by civilization.[5]

Edith was completely free behind her façade of technical virtuosity and abstraction, and in order to receive the images or understand the poetry I think it is necessary to abandon convention and try to transport oneself to the childhood level and ways of acceptance as the artist herself has done. 'If some of the images in these poems appear strange,' she said, 'it is because my senses are like those of primitive peoples, at once acute and uncovered – and they are interchangeable. Where the language of one sense is insufficient to convey a meaning, a sensation, I use another.'[6]

To begin a detailed study of each poem – not for its technical aspects of rhythm or sound, but for its meaning, its choice of words, its various levels of sense – was like being faced with a difficult jig-saw puzzle where, once the crucial piece is found and slipped into place, the rest of the picture suddenly fits together simply and logically. As I read through the poems of *Façade*, it was Edith's extraordinarily vivid imagery which conjured up for me a picture or scene which I have attempted to describe or interpret in its immediacy as a short story placed (in italic type) after each poem. This visual impression, while remaining essentially abstract like the poems, draws its setting and characters from the biographical allusions inherent in each poem. I hope that by reading the story with the poem we are able to see how Edith Sitwell, through her dissociation of ideas, escapes the

[4] Ibid., pp. 19-20.   [5] Ibid., pp. 20-1.
[6] Edith Sitwell, *Selected Poems* – 'Notes on my own poetry' (1936), p. 23.

constraints imposed by society and her upbringing, thus attaining the freedom to express her innermost thoughts within the fantasy of her poetry.

The commentary I have placed after each 'scene' discloses the biographical background relevant to the poems, enlarging on specific incidents or characters and, while attempting to unravel some of the obscurities, reveals Edith's genius for writing on so many levels, while at the same time combining to form one entity.

It was interesting to me to see, as I became involved in writing these impressions and delving into biographical details, that I had in fact chanced upon some very appropriate stories. For instance, the child's rocking-horse has a great significance for me in 'Hornpipe' (I have always imagined *Façade* taking place through the eyes of a child, rocking to the music as it sees everything larger than life). Later I learnt that the rocking-horse was much loved by the Sitwell children,[7] as it stood sentinel outside the nursery, dappled and with one ear missing. It was almost as large as a real pony and so old that its presence could be seen in a painting of a previous generation of Sitwell children from 1826, although the children were forbidden to ride it alone since the death of an uncle who had supposedly fallen off and been killed.

Another coincidence is the story of 'Mariner Man' which takes place in a train, making use of the reflection in the window. In his autobiography,[8] Sacheverell Sitwell describes a similar scene, though I came upon the book only after writing the story.

Of course I must stress the fantasy of the scenes. The gardener in 'Tarantella' is based on the character as Edith presents him in the poem, and although the real gardener, Ernest de Taye, certainly tended his fruit and vegetables with a peculiar intensity, he was not necessarily quite as extreme in real life as the poem would imply. However, Edith's comment that her texts were often based on personal memory rather than general experience, and that the reader must therefore be excused for not understanding certain details,[9] seems to me to justify the idea of presenting

[7] Osbert Sitwell, *The Scarlet Tree* (1946), p. 38.
[8] Sacheverell Sitwell, *All Summer in a Day* (1926), p. 119.
[9] Edith Sitwell, *Selected Poems* – 'Notes on my own poetry' (1936), p. 25.

biographical details relevant to each poem as they occur so that the reader can appreciate the poetry in all its aspects.

'Neither the sadness nor the gaiety of these poems has been understood nor any underlying meaning'.[10] Previous commentary on Edith Sitwell's poetry has been devoted primarily to the amazing technical elements which she employed and was readily able to discuss in detail. That she rarely went into any deep personal explanation is typical of her character and it does not follow that there is nothing beneath the surface brilliance. For instance, of 'Gold Coast Customs' she said that the writing of the poem had caused her so much anguish that she was not prepared to re-live it by talking about it, and would confine herself to technical discussion only.[11]

This attitude is surely a common artistic process. On many occasions on talking to musicians or artists, I have found that they 'excuse' their intangible creativity, as it were, by attributing it to a type of instrument or technical aspect which, of course, while important for the skilled execution, does not necessarily relate to the real 'soul' or artistry which has singled them out in their field.

Edith's knowledge and command of the English language were amazing, and her power of observation and sensitivity to the plight and situation of others is revealed on more than one level in her poetry: Greek mythological references are placed parallel with ordinary life, with historical or family events and with different cultures. She claimed that her poetry was the direct result of her extraordinary upbringing, the effects of which remained throughout her life. It has been said that perhaps in old age and ill-health she exaggerated some of her early experiences, but we have only to read Osbert's accounts of their childhood written in the 1940s[12] to perceive the same clarity regarding Edith's treatment and it becomes obvious that her life was in no way an easy one.

[10] Letter from Edith Sitwell to John Lehmann, 22 May 1944.
[11] Edith Sitwell, *Selected Poems* – 'Notes on my own poetry' (1936), p. 47
[12] Osbert Sitwell, *Left Hand Right Hand* (1945), *The Scarlet Tree* (1946).

'I was influenced by the outer surroundings of my childhood.'[13] Edith's arrival into the world on 7 September 1887 was already an unhappy event, with her ill-matched parents, Sir George Sitwell and Lady Ida Denison preparing for, and only expecting, a son and heir. Added to this, as she grew older her unconventional looks – she was tall and thin with an aquiline nose – heightened her father's cold disapproval, and she was continually subjected to her mother's violent rages, all of which contributed to the feeling that she was unloved and unwanted – a 'changeling'.[14]

She took refuge with the numerous servants, in particular with her nurse, Davis, and her father's valet, Henry Moat. While helping to keep the necessary distance between parents and child, they were able to stir her active imagination with the unending stories and legends surrounding her home, Renishaw Hall in Derbyshire, and her family history.

Edith taught herself to read when she was four, finding a welcome escape from her isolation and loneliness in the fairy-tales of Grimm and Hans Andersen. Travels abroad – her 'adventures' – also made a lasting impression on the strangely sensitive child. The winter months were spent in Scarborough, where the wild raging sea, which she loved, and the inhabitants of the town – circus folk, gypsies, pedlars, beggars and fishermen – were a constant source of wonder. But it was during the summers that Edith, together with her two brothers, Osbert born in 1892, and Sacheverell born five years later, built up their own fantasy world within the seclusion of the woods, park and gardens of Renishaw, and it was here that she began to read her poetry to them and encourage their own writing.

Edith's education was left to a string of governesses, the last of whom was the intensely artistic Helen Rootham. She encouraged Edith's talent and love for music, as well as introducing her to the French Symbolists and the poetry of Swinburne, and under her influence and friendship Edith's confidence increased. After the publication of her first poem, 'Drowned Suns',[15] she broke away from the confines and stifling atmosphere at home and, with Helen as chaperone, set up a modest existence in London, their

[13] Edith Sitwell, *Taken Care Of* (1965), p. 47.
[14] Ibid., p. 20.   [15] *Daily Mirror*, 13 March 1913.

dingy Bayswater flat becoming a meeting place for literary and artistic London.

'We didn't mean to be avant-garde.'[16] In her writing, Edith had been experimenting with rhythms – likening her poetry to the Transcendental Studies of Liszt[17] – and it was at the instigation of her brothers, who had seen the Cocteau-Picasso-Satie Ballet *Parade* in Paris, that she set to work with the initially sceptical William Walton to form an entertainment combining words and music – 'for fun'.[18] The voice was to be treated as an instrument and, in order to be heard above the music, the poems were to be recited through a megaphone (or Sengerphone, after a Mr Senger who lent the 'instrument' which he had invented to help his voice to be heard when singing the off-stage role of Fafner in Wagner's *Ring*). To the shy, nervous Edith it was extremely daring to recite before her literary friends and so, to avoid embarrassment, the idea of a curtain was devised, behind which the whole event took place – thus 'de-personalizing the texts'.[19]

Façade was performed for the first time on 24 January 1922 in the drawing room of 2 Carlyle Square, the home of Osbert and Sacheverell. William Walton conducted the straggly band of musicians, who had to be sustained by sloe gin, and the rather bewildered audience was gratefully revived with hot rum punch afterwards in the dining-room. The following year, after much consultation and substitution of poems, the first public performance took place at the Aeolian Hall. It caused such an immediate reaction of hostility or rage, that the Sitwells knew they had made a mark on the arts in some form or other. While Edith, dressed in her customary 'Gothic' style,[20] was basking in the limelight at the party afterwards – her friends around her playing charades – the newspaper reviewers were preparing their attack which would create the scandal establishing the Sitwell

[16] *Sunday Times*, 8 September 1957 – interview with Cyril Connolly.
[17] Edith Sitwell, *Taken Care Of* (1965), p. 123.
[18] Elizabeth Salter, *Last Years of a Rebel* (1967), p. 67.
[19] *Daily Mail*, 13 June 1923.
[20] Osbert Sitwell, *The Scarlet Tree* (1946), p. 230.

'cult' image for the rest of their lives. In the light of her first volumes of poetry, for which Edith had been unanimously hailed as a serious poet of great promise (although her controversial annual periodical *Wheels*, 1916-21, where she championed various poets as well as writing herself, caused no little discussion among critics), these *Façade* poems, more nonsense than sense,[21] bouncing along to popular ditties, foxtrots and tangos, must have seemed a strange deviation.

However, by 1926 *Façade* was acclaimed and assured a permanent place in the concert repertoire, although it was not till 1942 that the final choice of poems was established and 1951 that the definitive score was published.

'Almost all my poems are about the growth of consciousness'.[22] Edith's poetry is essentially of the mind. Her visual sense did not evolve from looking at paintings or sculpture, but by 'imagining'. Her pictures were running through her own head, which meant that her means of expressing what she saw came straight from within, making the impression totally personal. Edith's brother Sacheverell, translating her poetry to a visual medium, compared *Façade* to the *Balli di Sfessania* of Jacques Callot – a frontispiece and twenty-three woodcuts made in 1621-2, exactly three hundred years before *Façade* – and it is from these engravings that I have selected the illustrations for this book. Their appropriateness indicates their timeless fantasy and clarity which, like the poems, directly reflect the historical as well as the everyday events of their time.

Osbert relates[23] how the many wayward wanderers and minstrels on the seafront at Scarborough reminded him of Callot etchings as their voices were whipped away by the wind, leaving only their silent, bizarre attitudes, and Edith uses the names of Commedia dell' Arte figures in some of the poems of *Façade*, such as 'Captain Fracasse and Il Capitaneo'.

Like Edith, Callot was born into a prosperous family of

[21] Osbert Sitwell, *Laughter in the Next Room* (1949), pp. 192-3.
[22] Letter from Edith Sitwell to Allanah Harper, *c.* 1928.
[23] Osbert Sitwell, *Left Hand Right Hand* (1945), p. 82.

ennobled bourgeois. He enjoyed close contact with theatrical pomp and formality after becoming an apprentice metal engraver at the court of Charles III, where pageants, fêtes and ceremonies were the order of the day. Rebelling against his comfortable life, he ran away to Italy, joining a band of gypsies, and it was here that he observed the poses and theatrical gestures used in the Commedia dell' Arte. He is said to have modelled his figures for the *Balli di Sfessania* on a Maltese dance (known as 'sfessania' in Naples), which he encountered during a sea journey in 1620, while travelling from Livorno to Sicily.

The drawing opposite the title page describes the popular fair at Frescennia, with its numerous wandering actors, acrobats and charlatans. The division of the curtain at the back of the stage into three sections was typical for the wandering theatre groups of the time, and seems to me to symbolize very well the original curtain behind which the performances of *Façade* took place. A comparison between Edith's *Façade* poems and Callot's etchings is explicitly drawn in this extract from Sacheverell Sitwell's poem 'The Octogenarian':[24]

Poems in a vein of fantasy
    invented for yourself,
And all your own,
    like nothing else before or since

Excepting, I have often thought,
    a resemblance, even a kinship
To the *Balli di Sfessania* of Jacques Callot,
Who in the staid language of the dictionary of painters
    ran away from home at Nancy in Lorraine
And went to Rome,
'Some time between 1608-11*, aged fifteen or sixteen',
Having joined the Gypsies, or at least frequented
    fairgrounds and the encampments of nomad actors:–

---

[24] Sacheverell Sitwell, *An Indian Summer* (1964), p. 15.

* Within the lifetime of Shakespeare, as long ago as that.

Introduction

Jacques Callot being a youth of the precocity
        and youthful genius
Of the child Rimbaud another native of Lorraine

Of which experiences
        expressed in fantasy
The *Balli di Sfessania* are the memory;
A frontispiece and twenty-three little woodcuts of dancing figures
        no more than three or four inches high;
Giving the impression, I have tried to express it,
        as though he made the woodcuts using the point of his knife
Upon anything he could find,
        a wooden bench, the corner of a trestle-stage or kitchen
    table:–
And most improbably made the prints for them there and then,
        using what scraps of paper came to hand

Should one see all thirty-seven poems[25] of *Façade*
        printed close together on a theatre or concert programme,
The images jump at the eye off the crowded page
        in a strength of originality only reminiscent
Of the little woodcuts of the *Balli di Sfessania*

. . .

And I know it is incongruous,
        but in their femininity
They only match the masculine virility
        of the little woodcuts of the Rimbaud-youth,
Jacques Callot.

Façade – Parade – Charade: nothing is as it appears. From behind
her façade, Edith Sitwell evoked a mythical public image of
eccentricity which was partly brought out by her mode of dress –
she claimed that she looked ridiculous in the 'normal' fashion of
the day – and partly by her aggressive defensiveness which
became a necessity when she felt she was being misunderstood

[25] Cf. Preface above p. v.

artistically. Her sense of justice made her merciless to her enemies, although even her most avid critics, when closely questioned, would not refute her innate dignity and good breeding.

However, it was her acute perception and sensitivity that sharpened her experiences and observations of life in the early years of the twentieth century which emerge in her poems as a kaleidoscope of words and images.

The public Edith, the 'modern' cult figure, overshadowed the private poet, to such an extent that many people who are confident in their knowledge of her as a person confess to never having actually *read* her poetry with any seriousness. Perhaps this book may change this attitude. Of course it must be stressed that this work is simply *my* impression of *Façade*. The ultimate goal is to *enjoy* the poetry and if I can achieve my aim of bringing a lucidity to the complexity of the meanings behind Edith Sitwell's writing, I am certain that the experience for the reader will prove as illuminating as it has been for me – resulting in a heightened appreciation and fascination for both the woman and her art.

'But Cinderella has started on her journey; she will arrive at the ball and her beauty will be surpassing.'[26]

---

[26] Osbert Sitwell, *Who Killed Cock Robin?* (1921), p. 32.

1. Hornpipe

1. Hornpipe

Sailors come
To the drum
Out of Babylon;
Hobby-horses
Foam, the dumb
Sky rhinoceros-glum

Watched the courses of the breakers' rocking-horses and with
Glaucis,
Lady Venus on the settee of the horsehair sea!
Where Lord Tennyson in laurels wrote a gloria free,
In a borealic iceberg came Victoria; she
Knew Prince Albert's tall memorial took the colours of the floreal
And the borealic iceberg; floating on they see
New-arisen Madam Venus for whose sake from far
Came the fat and zebra'd emperor from Zanzibar
Where like golden bouquets lay far Asia, Africa, Cathay,
All laid before that shady lady by the fibroid Shah.
Captain Fracasse stout as any water-butt came, stood
With Sir Bacchus both a-drinking the black tarr'd grapes' blood
Plucked among the tartan leafage
By the furry wind whose grief age
Could not wither – like a squirrel with a gold star-nut.
Queen Victoria sitting shocked upon the rocking horse
Of a wave said to the Laureate, 'This minx of course
Is as sharp as any lynx and blacker-deeper than the drinks and
quite as
Hot as any hottentot, without remorse!
                    For the minx',
                          Said she,
                'And the drinks,
                          You can see
Are hot as any hottentot and not the goods for me!'

1. Hornpipe

There is a slight creaking as the old horse rocks to and fro, the safety in its worn, rough mane and familiar long neck obscuring a direct view to the centre of the darkening room. Through half-closed eyes the white lace curtains may be the foam edging backwards and forwards on the sands, soothing and reassuring in its rhythm. But the freshening wind is missing.

In the drawing-room they are still taking tea, the sofa and chairs grouped intimately in the richly furnished room, the stern ancestral pictures reminding them constantly of the family bond which unites such varying temperaments and characters, the old and the young. Only the exotic wall-tapestries give a hint of a different life: strange colours, birds, giant-like foliage, dark figures, enticing folds of smooth silk and brocade.

The social occasion is deemed as meaningless as any other, the poker-faced figures grasping at the well-worn topics, conforming to the safe and the acceptable – to anything indeed, as long as it does not betray the real thoughts, real feelings that each member of the group must harbour, however unwillingly.

The men of the world, always restless, stand by the huge fireplace and, warmed also by alcohol, inevitably revert to their usual themes: the acts of daring (albeit at this distance a mingling of fact and fantasy), the 'fast living' and indulgence they once enjoyed in the name of Colonial Benevolence.

The female members of the company have only one way to relieve the frustration: the complete denouncement of life in general and its all too numerous vices – alcohol and the carnal pleasures. Of course they have no experience, but one hears so much!

Smugness takes over.

One must always be on one's guard.

All tendencies to enjoy life's pleasures must be discouraged at all costs.

Meanwhile, to alleviate the boredom: 'Come here and amuse us, child!'

The rocking horse wavers, and then is still.

1. Hornpipe

The story of *Façade* begins with a Hornpipe. As we accompany Edith through her colourful world of thoughts and experiences we assemble in the Great Drawing Room at Renishaw. This room, and what it represents, provides the link between the two main themes which pervade all the *Façade* poems: the contrast of Victorian Aristocratic Life – its stiffness, restriction and seeming emotional paralysis – with the Sea – symbol of freedom, space, movement, adventure and fantasy.

Seated in the drawing-room one might have found Grandmother Sitwell and her daughter Florence, whose unbounded religious fervour contrasted with grandmother Londesborough's palatial life-style and appreciation of worldly pleasures. (Her husband's pleasures extended to entertaining actresses from the music-halls at every opportunity.)

Various other lesser (poorer) relations would always be present, known collectively as the 'fun brigade', laughing when nothing better offered in order to please Lady Ida, practising false kindness on the children, when necessary, and thus being assured of the invitation for a lengthy visit next season.

The centrepiece is the Sitwell Family Portrait by Sargent – in itself a façade – with Sir George in riding habit, although he never rode, and Lady Ida, pretty in a ball-gown and hat, pretending to arrange flowers. While her brothers play, the thirteen-year-old Edith looks down from the picture with an uncanny strength and awareness of this intimate family illusion.

The Victorian era changed in 1861 on the death of Albert ('memorial') from one of sweetness and flowers ('colours of the floreal') to the frosty stiffness (brought by 'Boreas', the north wind).

Queen Victoria, like Albert, greatly admired Tennyson, and made him Poet Laureate. After Albert's death she kept a copy of his works by her bed.

All is not as it seems; the Victorian rigidity and control on the surface in the drawing-room belies the human frailty beneath, which the characters in 'Hornpipe' reflect.

The drum represents the beating of time and emphasizes the reforming spirit of the age calling to repentance before it is too late. The disintegration of Babylon refers to the dissipated life.

22

1. Hornpipe

Venus was unfaithful to her husband, Vulcan, and loved, among others, Bacchus, the god of wine who, though effeminate and beautiful, was given to bouts of revelry. With Captain Fracasse, he represents fast living. The 'black tarr'd grapes' blood' refer to whisky, and the 'furry wind whose grief age could not wither' implies that deposits of alcohol only improve with age in the bottle. With such a gathering, appearances must always be maintained and the self-righteous abnegation of worldly indulgences was the only course to follow, implying that all other forms of behaviour were beneath discussion ('hottentot'). One had to look to lands abroad – Persia, China – to enjoy in peace the freedom and dubious pleasures, in particular with the sharp-eyed ('lynx') amoral women ('minx').

Edith contrasts the colours of gold, which emphasizes wealth and luxury ('golden bouquets', 'gold star-nut') and black, which means the immoral life ('shady lady' and 'minx blacker than the drinks'). The 'zebra'd emperor', resplendent in rich clothes, combines his wealth ('gold') with dark skin and amoral living. Edith described her wealthy Grandmother Londesborough as living like a gilded wasp (also striped).[1] The 'fibroid Shah' suggests the decadence of the Persian leader as he indulges his passions freely.

The drawing-room and the sea are linked by the numerous horses: sea-horse and horse-hair sofa; high horse, representing the drawing-room attitude; and hobby horse, the movement of the waves. But of course most important is the sailor's dance – the hornpipe – a dance for pleasure, but not a closely communicative one: a hornpipe is danced alone.

[1] *The New Age Readers and Writers*, July 1922.

2. En Famille

2. En Famille

In the early spring-time, after their tea,
Through the young fields of the springing Bohea,
Jemima, Jocasta, Dinah, and Deb
Walked with their father Sir Joshua Jebb –
An admiral red, whose only notion,
(A butterfly poised on a pigtailed ocean)
Is of the peruked sea whose swell
Breaks on the flowerless rocks of Hell.
Under the thin trees, Deb and Dinah,
Jemima, Jocasta, walked, and finer
Their black hair seemed (flat-sleek to see)
Than the young leaves of the springing Bohea;
Their cheeks were like nutmeg-flowers when swells
The rain into foolish silver bells.
They said, 'If the door you would only slam,
Or if, Papa, you would once say "Damn" –
Instead of merely roaring "Avast"
Or boldly invoking the nautical Blast –
We should now stand in the street of Hell
Watching siesta shutters that fell
With a noise like amber softly sliding;
Our moon-like glances through these gliding
Would see at her table preened and set
Myrrhina sitting at her toilette
With eyelids closed as soft as the breeze
That flows from gold flowers on the incense-trees.'

. . .

The Admiral said, 'You could never call –
I assure you it would not do at all!
She gets down from table without saying "Please",
Forgets her prayers and to cross her T's,
In short, her scandalous reputation
Has shocked the whole of the Hellish nation;
And every turbaned Chinoiserie,
With whom we should sip our black Bohea,

25

2. En Famille

Would stretch out her simian fingers thin
To scratch you, my dears, like a mandoline;
For Hell is just as properly proper
As Greenwich, or as Bath, or Joppa!'

The family afternoon walk is a peaceful idyll. The Head of the Household strolls with his daughters along the neat pathways, past the formal flower-beds and out into the park. The English gentleman at home is fortunate in being able to command time with his children. Such a harmonious existence can only be envied – at least from a distance.

They walk in silence, seemingly oblivious to the first signs of growth and tentative green, the large naval figure leading – strong, impenetrable, with his mind far away, recalling the freedom and adventure of his former life at sea. The girls follow, two by two, exquisitely dressed in sailor collars, button boots and demure hats, which safely hide the blatant signs of approaching womanhood. Only the unmistakable glow of their faces reflects their thoughts and secrets (the result of endless burning discussions among themselves) and anticipates the excitement and pleasures that growing up will bring. If only Father would unbend a little, listen and try to understand what is happening within their bodies and minds!

Gaining courage by the feeling that spring and change are in the air, and far away from the confines of the stiff and formal rooms of the house, they grow bolder. They dare to think they might venture to explain their feelings and wishes (so difficult to account for even to themselves). They are grown up and have minds of their own. They are ready to 'come out' in Society and taste the freedom that other young women of their age and distinction enjoy.

But no! He knows best. The world is full of evil. Wickedness lurks in all levels of society. They cannot understand the danger. He must protect his little girls from folly. It is his duty. He cannot allow them to be tainted and tarnished. He knows the pitfalls only too well ...

They have no choice. Their upbringing has seen to that! There

2. En Famille

is nothing left but total submission and obedience – and the world of daydreams.

As a child, Edith's unloved position with her parents forced her to rely on her own fantasy, in an increased feeling for nature and animals. She loved her griffon, Dido, and when she was five years old enjoyed an intense relationship with a peacock. This strange creature remained loyal, waiting for her every morning to come out into the garden, until Sir George bought a mate of its own species and Edith was left cruelly abandoned.

Growing up was a difficult task under the total domination of her father, who considered his opinions infallible. He was a learned, solitary man who wrote books on gardens and a family history. Edith was in many ways very like him, with her gift for detail and her single-mindedness. He insisted that her interests and accomplishments should follow *his* expectations: drawing classes, though she showed no aptitude; learning the cello, which she hated; going to the races as a treat. According to Osbert, a more complete mismanagement of a human being could scarcely be imagined.[1]

Sir George spent a great deal of time in the vast grounds of Renishaw, pacing up and down, muttering to himself, as he measured and planned new additions and changes – statues, waterfalls or new vistas. He was less interested in flowers, or colour, than in architectural proportions.

It is early spring in the formal gardens. The seasons play an important role in setting mood in all the poems of *Façade*, and here spring represents the tentative awakening from childhood to womanhood. Edith's continual reference to beauty, in particular hair ('the peruked sea'), is a natural preoccupation with the attributes she felt she lacked completely. Also, the degrading *beautifying* devices (nose- and back-straighteners), which her parents inflicted upon her as a child, caused permanent damage, not only to her nose and back, but to her self-esteem.

The poem takes place out of doors, which may make the

[1] Osbert Sitwell, *Left Hand Right Hand* (1945), p. 90.

attempt to communicate easier than it would be within the confines of four walls. The nautical link (the 'Admiral'), emphasizes the supreme authority, as well as the freedom, that the naval life makes possible. 'Avast' (stop), 'Bohea' (low-grade tea in China) and 'the butterfly on the pigtailed ocean' (the sailing ship in the China seas) all indicate that Edith longed to discover life's secrets for herself. 'Myrrhina': exotic, aromatic, diffuse sensuality.

Every society has its rules, whether it be Bath or Joppa.

3. Mariner Man

3. Mariner Man

'What are you staring at, mariner man
Wrinkled as sea-sand and old as the sea?'
'Those trains will run over their tails, if they can,
Snorting and sporting like porpoises. Flee
The burly, the whirligig wheels of the train,
As round as the world and as large again,
Running half the way over to Babylon, down
Through fields of clover to gay Troy town –
A-puffing their smoke as grey as the curl
On my forehead as wrinkled as sands of the sea! –
But what can that matter to you, my girl?
(And what can that matter to me?)'

*The darkening shapes of the hills, barely distinguishable in the
evening mist and the monotonous rhythm of the wheels, have
gradually lulled the occupants of the compartment into a limp
sleep, their faces, yellow-lit from the dim bulb overhead, strange
and inanimate. Only the nautical figure seated by the door, whose
taut body has resisted every jolt and sway since the journey
began, and the tall, thin, intense child next to the window
opposite have not succumbed to the inevitable state of oblivion.*

*She is fascinated by his rough, strong, weather-beaten face
with clouded eyes staring intently out of the window. What can
he see? What are his thoughts? He seems to be drawn forward as
if against his will. Does he not want to make the journey? Is he
still thinking of the sea? With every second they leave it further
and further behind, as each turn of the powerful wheels brings
the big city nearer and the beginning of something new, unknown
– the future.*

*She looks at her reflection in the window, wide-eyed with
anticipation and excitement. Suddenly he looms before her as the
train in a noisy, steamy swirl rushes into the tunnel. His face fills
the glass, leaving her own small image just visible in the corner.*

*As she looks directly at him, his gaze fixes on her, and just for a
second she catches a faint, quizzical gleam in his eyes. Then he is*

30

gone. The noise abates and the swirling mists retreat to a safer distance.

She will never know his secret. Despite their close proximity, as they hurtle along the straight iron tracks to the same destination, each is alone.

The dreams of the young contrast sharply with those of the old. Edith watches the old sailor. Her interest in the sea stemmed from her early childhood in Scarborough and was further kindled by the endless seafaring stories told by her father's valet, Henry Moat, whose family came from a long line of whalers.

The sailor looks back on his life as it nears its end. The smoke from the train compares with the mist on the sea (also the smog from the coal-mines surrounding Renishaw) and spreads a haze over the sailor's life, the memories becoming fainter with the passing of time. The wheels of the train move relentlessly (time moves so fast when one is old). They represent the movement and change from the world of the country-side to a mechanical, material universe.

The city of Babylon (life) is disintegrating, crumbling into insignificance for the sailor; but for Edith Troy was the city of pleasure. She named her grandmother's house in Wales Troy Park, and though she had never been there it became a symbol in her imagination for the life of happiness and pleasure which she could not experience.

4. Long Steel Grass

4. Long Steel Grass

Long steel grass –
The white soldiers pass –
The light is braying like an ass.
See
The tall Spanish jade
With hair black as nightshade
Worn as a cockade!
Flee
Her eyes' gasconade
And her gown's parade
(As stiff as a brigade).
Tee-hee!
The hard and braying light
is zebra'd black and white
It will take away the slight
And free,
Tinge of the mouth-organ sound,
(Oyster-stall notes) oozing round
Her flounces as they sweep the ground.
The
Trumpet and the drum
And the martial cornet come
To make the people dumb –
But we
Won't wait for sly-foot night
(Moonlight, watered milk-white, bright)
To make clear the declaration
Of our Paphian vocation,
Beside the castanetted sea,
Where stalks Il Capitaneo
Swaggart braggadocio
Sword and moustachio –

* ' "Long Steel Grass" is in fact called "Trio for two cats and a Trombone". It is about a couple of cats, do you see, having a love affair.' Edith Sitwell, *Last Years of a Rebel*, p. 182.

4. Long Steel Grass

He
Is green as a cassada
And his hair is an armada.
To the jade 'Come kiss me harder'
He called across the battlements as she
Heard our voices thin and shrill
As the steely grasses' thrill,
Or the sound of the onycha
When the phoca has the pica
In the palace of the Queen Chinee!

*Olive skin, flashing eyes, clothing scant and sensuous condense to
form the dark, rhythmical shadow pacing the white-hot ground.*
  Tempting.
*High on the parapet, the colourful, uniformed silhouettes in
formation are etched against the deep brilliant sky. Puppet-like
movements: forwards/backwards, slow, drilled.*
The water surrounding the walls glints in the sun.
The castle railings are hard and forbidding.
  Separating.
*Under the orange trees a towsled man pauses, his hand caressing
the smooth black onyx figure. Then, sliding it gently to the corner
of the stone-chequered table, he releases his hold and settles back.*
  Watching.
*His companion, wasp-like from the shadows of the railing, places
his ivory piece with deliberate care.*
  Provoking.
*The body of men descends the stronghold, slows to a halt by the
tall gates and then disperses. The strategist remains. He will play.*
*The distorted sounds of amusement issuing through the narrow
slits in the walls of the castle diffuse the false words of passion
quivering in the motionless air.*
  Flirting.
*The towsled man at the table, with a swift movement, removes the
ivory figure.*
  Conquering.
The game continues.

4. Long Steel Grass

Edith travelled a great deal with her parents from an early age, claiming to have had as many night train journeys as any girl her age; but when she was taken to Italy she was not interested in the usual sights, scrambling round Vesuvius, or in the principles of architecture in which her father wished to instruct her. Instead, she was fascinated by the children who played with abandon around the fish markets in Naples, bare-footed, laughing, looking for lice in their hair.

A new warmth emerges. Life in England differs from life abroad. Everything becomes clear-cut, and this poem becomes a story of contrasts: light and shade, man and woman, black and white, good and evil.

The railings seen as the 'long steel grass' are striped from the alternating sun and shadow, forming a barrier between the palace and the outer world – the two moral standards.

The soldier – 'Il Capitaneo' – stands white in the sun, socially acceptable; but the prostitute is black in the shadows – an outcast, inferior. 'Hair black as nightshade' and the (white) cockade – worn by the servants of the crown – evoke the contrast of the black-and-white berries of the deadly nightshade.

The 'Paphian vocation' (Venus was born in the island of Paphos) is the pursuit of love, and the deep-voiced male 'phoca' (seal) woos the jay ('pica'), the silly woman; but there is no sincerity. The sounds are distorted as they issue from the 'onycha' (mollusc shell). The male has the advantage in this game: she may seem confident, flaunting herself and boasting ('her eyes' gasconade', 'her gown's parade') like the soldier 'swaggart braggadocio', but she is considered the scum of the earth in the eyes of the world 'oyster-stall notes oozing'. She can never cross the barrier from her house of ill-repute ('palace of the Queen Chinee') to his palace – normal society.

5. Through Gilded Trellises

'Through gilded trellises
Of the heat, Dolores,
Inez, Manuccia,
Isabel, Lucia,
Mock Time that flies.
"Lovely bird, will you stay and sing,
Flirting your sheened wing, –
Peck with your beak, and cling
To our balconies?"
They flirt their fans, flaunting –
"O silence enchanting
As music!" then slanting
Their eyes,
Like gilded or emerald grapes,
They take mantillas, capes,
Hiding their simian shapes.
Sighs
Each lady, "Our spadille
Is done." ... "Dance the quadrille
From Hell's towers to Seville;
Surprise
Their siesta," Dolores
Said. Through gilded trellises
Of the heat, spangles
Pelt down through the tangles
Of bell-flowers; each dangles
Her castanets, shutters
Fall while the heat mutters,
With sounds like a mandoline
Or tinkled tambourine. ...
Ladies, Time dies!'

5. Through Gilded Trellises

The plateau is reached after the effort of the slow and dusty climb. The faint breeze immediately feels cool against the moist skin. It has been worth the effort. Beneath the luxuriant vines, the sunlight filters now and then between the wide leaves, filling the summerhouse with pools of light which remain motionless in the silent midday heat.

Sleep takes over.... Jerked into consciousness, the musicians have obviously resumed their task. The preening and parading have begun afresh, with nervous fans hiding expectant faces as they wait to be chosen by some handsome partner and whisked onto the ballroom floor, with all thoughts of the heat and crowds and discomfort forgotten, to be 'borne like a bird' until the fading music signals the return to earth.

They are the lucky ones, for whom the round of balls and social events means nothing but amusement and pleasure with the promise of a 'suitable husband' at the end of the season. For those unfortunates for whom not even the employment of masks and fans can have an improving effect, there is only the humiliation of securing a partner for nothing more than the interminable card game. And the evening wears on languidly, the heat more oppressive, until the indifferent displaying of the fan can no longer hide the boredom and shame of the crestfallen. Yet another evening ends like all the others. Time is getting on, youth does not remain forever....

Roused unwillingly from sleep, as if sensing the moment when the apathy of the day gives way to evening, the sandy ground is tinged golden in the setting sun and the darts of sunlight dance as the cooling wind fans the leaves.

A large bird flaps its wings as it flies overhead, black against the sky.

In the distance the faint sounds of strumming drift across the plain.

The afternoon has slipped away....

Inspired by his travels in Italy, Sir George bought a mediaeval castle, Montegufoni, in the Tuscan hills, where he could indulge his obsession with the details of mediaeval life.

5. Through Gilded Trellises

This poem combines a typically shaded terrace abroad with the ballroom at Londesborough in Scarborough, the home of Edith's wealthy maternal grandmother. The glitter ('spangles') of Spain contrasts with the English blue-and-white 'bell-flowers'.

The oppressive heat and boredom which affected Edith when she travelled abroad can be linked directly to the social awkwardness and the feeling of unattractiveness that made her dislike social activities like balls and banquets. Quadrille is both a dance and a card game, 'spadille' being the ace of spades in quadrille. From 'Hell's towers' (Renishaw's coal-mining chimneys) to 'Seville' (abroad) the same boredom is felt: life never changes.

Edith's preoccupation with the colours green and gold is evident in this poem with 'gilded or emerald grapes'; and the mocking bird has a literal significance ('mock Time that flies') as she watches the women imitating each other. As they dance, she likens them to the numerous parrots and cockatoos kept by her grandmother; and they would become just as flighty in their pursuit of pleasure, with fans spreading like a peacock's tail; whereas the Spanish women, despite the heat, were always at home in their bodies, their movements totally natural.

For Edith the shutters, trellis and fan were used to hide behind 'simian shapes' (monkey-like features), to keep cool and to guard her private world. 'Siesta' implies living one's life in comfortable oblivion hidden behind one's façade.

The hands move round the clockface slowly when one is bored.

6. Tango-Pasodoble

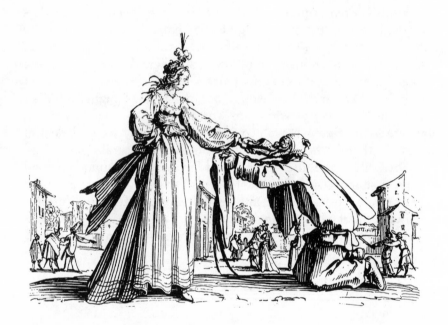

6. Tango-Pasodoble

When
                    Don
Paquito arrived at the seaside
Where the donkey's hide tide brayed, he
Saw the banditto Jo in a black cape
Whose slack shape waved like the sea –
Thetis wrote a treatise noting wheat is silver like the sea;
    the lovely cheat is sweet as foam; Erotis notices that she
                    Will
                    Steal
                    The
Wheat-king's luggage, like Babel
Before the League of Nations grew –
So Jo put the luggage and the label
In the pocket of Flo the Kangaroo.
Through trees like rich hotels that bode
Of dreamless ease fled she,
Carrying the load and goading the road
Through the marine scene to the sea.
'Don Pasquito, the road is eloping
With your luggage, though heavy and large;
You must follow and leave your moping
Bride to my guidance and charge!'

When
                    Don
Pasquito returned from the road's end,
Where vanilla-coloured ladies ride
From Sevilla, his mantilla'd bride and young friend
Were forgetting their mentor and guide.
For the lady and her friend from Le Touquet
In the very shady trees upon the sand
Were plucking a white satin bouquet
Of foam, while the sand's brassy band
Blared in the wind. Don Pasquito

41

6. Tango-Pasodoble

Hid where the leaves drip with sweet ...
But a word stung him like a mosquito ...
For what they hear, they repeat!

The chequered sky cannot decide whether to paint the sea blue or grey. Every few minutes the whole vista changes, alternating between a typical summer scene and the rather dreary picture of holiday-makers determined to make the most of their day at the seaside.

To the thin, pale girl proudly resting on the arm of the soldier, it makes no difference – as long as she can parade along the front in her new, summery dress and know that everyone will stare and think what a fine couple they make.

It happened like that in the restaurant when he arrived to collect her the day before the wedding. She hadn't finished with two tables; so he sat down, like any other customer, looking so smart in his uniform, and she felt her cheeks burn with pride as all the other waitresses studied him – and envied her.

But now she can look forward to the day stretching ahead: no more thoughts of tea-trays and half-eaten sandwiches which were her daily routine. They walk the length of the beach in silence, bare-footed, clutching their shoes, and then retrace their steps slowly, the water dragging at their ankles. She doesn't notice him at first – the tall, dark figure approaching the water's edge. When he is near enough to speak he beckons to the young man at her side, and after a few hurried words they go to her. He must return to the barracks immediately, but he won't be gone long and meanwhile his 'camerade' will look after her and keep her amused.

It is colder. The wind has gathered momentum and the grey light is beginning to fade before he arrives at the beach again. He looks around him. Apart from an old fisherman or two, the beach is deserted.

He heads for the far end where the dark rocks jut into the water, now that the tide has begun to wend its way inland.

He stops still. All too familiar sounds are issuing from behind the largest, smooth rock. He cannot move. Frozen and numb, he stands rooted, listening.

He cannot tear himself away.

6. Tango-Pasodoble

This poem is in a sense the reverse of the last, which was set abroad (in Spain) with thoughts of England. It takes place at a typical seaside resort (Scarborough), and Edith Sitwell has often described in her writings the simple Bank Holiday scene: people paddling, shrimping, riding donkeys, watching a Punch and Judy show or eating winkles while the brass band plays on the sea-front.[1]

This all conveys a comfortable security, with the 'League of Nations' formed in 1920 for the promotion of peace, or the Joey safely tucked into its mother's pouch.

However, as the title suggests, all is not quite so innocent; the darker, Latin, foreign tango points to something sinister beneath the apparent simplicity, and the tension caused by these contrasting elements results in activity (the tango being a strong Latin dance). The difference between Spain and England is emphasized by 'Babel': the confusion of tongues meaning the inability to communicate due to total lack of understanding.

The characters are straightforward and clear: Don Pasquito, the soldier, naive and genuinely in love with his bride (the nymph Thetis given in marriage against her will – the deception of the marriage state); his girl, seemingly ingenuous, and the 'banditto Jo', the deceiver ('Erotis', the loved one).

This last was surely a role for Wyndham Lewis, the only man who had a strong physical interest in Edith. She sat to him every day for ten months, and during the portrait sessions he would assume various characters, as the mood took him. A favourite was the Spanish role, as Edith called it, when he would dress up in a cape and huge black hat – every bit the dark 'banditto'. Eventually his attentions became unbearable to her and she refused to sit to him any more, leaving the portrait unfinished. They became enemies, resorting to the written word as weapons of attack.

This poem is a simple story of newly-weds – of their fickle passions and ultimate infidelity.

[1] Edith Sitwell, *Taken Care Of* (1965), p. 161.

7. Lullaby for Jumbo

Jumbo asleep!
Grey leaves thick-furred
As his ears, keep
Conversations blurred.
Thicker than hide
Is the trumpeting water;
Don Pasquito's bride
And his youngest daughter
Watch the leaves
Elephantine grey:
What is it grieves
In the torrid day?
Is it the animal
World that snores
Harsh and inimical
In sleepy pores? –
And why should the spined flowers
Red as a soldier
Make Don Pasquito
Seem still mouldier?

*Dawn. The steamy mist is grey, warm, moist. The faint throbbing
of the enormous vessel disturbs the thick, motionless water.*

*The line of land is still invisible. The sensuous fragrance of the
hot, steamy vegetation reaches the nostrils. Later the heat of the
sun dries out the dampness, but the mildew has destroyed the
beauty.*

Can the journey revive a dwindling marriage?
Time slowly rots, decays.
Regrets.
Only dreams bring respite.

Edith travelled as much by sea as by train, and as a child always
imagined the steamers to be elephants ('Jumbo') with their

trumpeting sirens, their trunks serving as funnels, 'thick-furred' meaning strong and sturdy (double-planked) ships.

The vibration of the engine forms the background to any words spoken ('conversations blurred'). Edith and her mother, who always needed fresh air, would spend time on deck during a sea crossing. Sir George remained solitary as usual, stretched out on a sofa in the stuffiest of the public rooms below.

Owing to their clash of temperaments, Lady Ida and Sir George had an unsatisfactory relationship, and the boredom and incompatibility would be exaggerated by the lack of space and diversion on board ship.

The 'lullaby', or gentle rocking motion, combined with the heat ('torrid day') and the humidity ('sleepy pores'), caused drowsiness and an escape from reality in sleep or dreams. Even the brilliant tropical flowers on the shore deceive: 'spined flowers' imply decay, and the boring and dull ('mouldier') Don Pasquito appears to suffer from swine fever ('red soldier') which causes a reddening of the skin.

Edith wrote[1] that she imagined crossing the lake at Renishaw in a toy steamer, and then walking through the hot-houses among the rare exotic plants which the Flemish gardener, Ernest de Taye, cared for so lovingly.

[1] Edith Sitwell, *Children's Tales from the Russian Ballet Retold* (1920), pp. 16-17.

8. Black Mrs Behemoth

In a room of the palace
Black Mrs Behemoth
Gave way to wroth
And the wildest malice.
Cried Mrs Behemoth,
'Come, come,
Come, court lady,
Doomed like a moth,
Through palace rooms shady!'
The candle flame
Seemed a yellow pompion,
Sharp as a scorpion,
Nobody came ...
Only a bugbear
Air unkind,
That bud-furred papoose,
The young spring wind,
Blew out the candle.
Where is it gone?
To flat Coromandel
Rolling on!

Is it a footstep that disturbs? There is silence in the room as the thin, wan child sits up wildly, the flowing blonde hair covering the white of her gown. The small casement-window allows the curve of the moon to alleviate the pitch black by streaking across the stone floor, transforming the heavy oak furniture into huge forbidding shapes.

The child climbs from the high bed, and walks noiselessly towards the door and out into the dark passage. She glides along, white and briefly luminous as she passes each window, and then down the stairs with considered steps, her feet never faltering, the pale eyes wide open.

At the far end of the house, the old housekeeper is preparing to retire for her short night. She has re-arranged the piles of linen

8. Black Mrs Behemoth

for her charge. The child is simply unable to execute the neat stitches that are an essential part of her education, so it is going to be even more difficult tomorrow, when she will have to re-do all the work of the previous day, until it is perfect – no matter how long that will take!

The child is useless in the house with her awkwardness: unable to please the ladies, unable to please in the kitchens. In fact, it is only the promise made to her sister on her death-bed, to care for the unwanted child, that forces her to bother with her at all, and anyway it all seems in vain: the child has learnt nothing, no matter what threats and punishments are meted out. But she will not give up yet!

She picks up the candle and sets off deliberately up the stairs. The white-clad figure stands fearlessly in the shadows as the old woman passes by. Then she follows at a distance, her bare feet making no sound. As the old lady opens her own heavy door, she turns, candle in hand, but the corridor is suddenly black. The draughty wind at the top of the house protects the child as she passes into her room, crosses the moonlight and climbs back to bed.

Her eyes close as her head touches the pillow.

It was through the servants, and the seclusion of the gardens, that Edith escaped notice, avoiding her mother's erratic temper and consequent rages, which could flare up at any moment. Lady Ida had been treated the same way by her own mother, the Countess of Londesborough, a formidable woman. Osbert noted[1] how his mother and her sisters trembled before her even as adults.

Lady Ida needed friends and relations around her for diversion, and they flocked – her generosity was infamous. But it was these guests who encouraged her rages, applauding her afterwards and taunting her whenever they could to make Edith the centre of their fun.

This was bad enough for Edith, sensitive as she was. It was also difficult for her to bear the contrasting behaviour towards her

---

[1] Osbert Sitwell, *Left Hand Right Hand* (1945), pp. 139-140, *The Scarlet Tree* (1946), p. 22.

49

brothers, who were loved and favoured. As a result, perhaps, an extraordinary bond of loyalty and friendship grew up between them all, and the fantasy world in which they loved to retreat became important.

Edith's conception of her mother was of a 'Behemoth' – a huge creature (hippopotamus) – whom she saw as frightening, seeking her out, and then playing with her. Edith was like a moth dancing round a candle, trapped and enticed by the flame – totally powerless.

The 'yellow pompion' (pumpkin) implies that the candle takes on a bigger dimension in the eyes of the frightened child (yellow being a type of moth).

The 'scorpion' was a whip with metal points, used in Biblical times. 'Bugbear' was the sixteenth-century term for an imaginary object of fear. 'Papoose', a North-American Indian child ('bud-furred', not yet developed) and 'young spring wind' both indicate the same lack of strength.

The only wish is to escape as far as possible: to 'Coromandel', the eastern seaboard of India.

The complete darkness ('blew out the candle') allowed Edith to escape her mother's wrath, but it also refers to another servant, Stephen Pare, who was blinded after being struck by lightning. Despite his disability, he would polish the silver candlesticks until they shone and had never been known to place any object incorrectly.

9. Tarantella

9. Tarantella

Where the satyrs are chattering, nymphs with their flattering
Glimpse of the forest enhance
All the beauty of marrow and cucumber narrow
And Ceres will join in the dance.
Where the satyrs can flatter the flat-leaved fruit
And the gherkin green and the marrow,
Said Queen Venus, 'Silenus, we'll settle between us
The gourd and the cucumber narrow.'
See, like palaces hid in the lake, they shake –
Those greenhouses shot by her arrow narrow!
The gardener seizes the pieces, like Croesus, for gilding the
    potting-shed barrow.
There the radish roots,
And the strawberry fruits
Feel the nymphs' high boots in the glade.
Trampling and sampling mazurkas, cachucas and turkas,
Cracoviaks hid in the shade.
Where, in the haycocks, the country nymphs' gay flocks
Wear gowns that are looped over bright yellow petticoats,
Gaiters of leather and pheasants' tail feathers
In straw hats bewildering many a leathern bat.
There they haymake,
Cowers and whines in showers
The dew in the dogskin bright flowers;
Pumpkin and marrow
And cucumber narrow
Have grown through the spangled June hours.
Melons as dark as caves have for their fountain waves
Thickest gold honey. And wrinkled as dark as Pan,
Or old Silenus, yet youthful as Venus
Are gourds and the wrinkled figs
Whence all the jewels ran.
Said Queen Venus, 'Silenus
We'll settle between us
The nymphs' disobedience, forestall

9. Tarantella

With my bow and my quiver
Each fresh evil liver:
For I don't understand it at all!'

We do it on purpose, I think. He is always to be seen in his steamy hot-houses, bending lovingly over his pots. We creep up and watch him. The glass glints in the sun and we can't always make him out from a distance, but we know he will be there.

Sometimes he stands motionless for minutes on end with a large, smooth marrow between his rough hands, or a basket of peaches before him, each one softer and more beautifully coloured than the next. I sometimes dare to step inside. Either he doesn't notice, as his glazed eyes stare down at his treasures, or he will suddenly lunge at me, stiff and strange but not frightening. It doesn't feel like a real threat, and we laugh and rush away to the woods.

I often wish I might stay and talk to him, be allowed to plunge my hands into the deep brown soil in the different-sized pots. It does smell wonderful in the greenhouse, damp and fresh. But he is unapproachable – the proud and silent king of his transparent castle.

We love the summer and the freedom to roam the gardens all day long in bright, easy dresses with straw hats shading our faces from the sun. We sit under the trees and gossip – waiting for our male companions to find us, as they always do; we make sure we are visible. Sometimes they creep up behind us and we run to another part of the gardens, crouching under bushes for cover. Sometimes in the ensuing excitement we take a short cut through the rows of vegetables, and the gardener leaves his greenhouse and slowly walks to the middle of the patch staring.

When we are caught after the frenzied chase and have willingly paid the customary penalty, he will still be staring – wondering, motionless: a scarecrow with man-made heart and a large green apron-pocket stuffed with cucumbers, his hands supporting a perfectly rounded and furrowed pumpkin.

9. Tarantella

'Tarantella': the strong desire or mania to pursue to extremes a particular objective.

The tarantella is a dance from Southern Italy (from Taranto) performed to the point of exhaustion, the remedy for the hysterical malady of tarantism being popularly attributed to the bite or sting of the tarantula spider. It can be compared to the frenzied lust of the gardener in the poem as he furtively observes the sexual abandon of the young country folk. He is left with his vegetables in the greenhouse, which consequently take on the giant-sized images of his frustrated dreams.

The poem begins with the 'satyrs' (the young men) who were the woodland gods in human form with goats' ears, tails, legs and budding horns). Dreaded by mortals (the gardener), and connected with the worship of Bacchus, they were fond of every sensual pleasure, particularly voluptuous dances with the nymphs. These were the semi-divine maidens inhabiting the woods or trees, and they represent the young, beautiful, half-naked women whom Silenus lusted after. He was the demi-god of drunkenness, wine, sleep and sensual living and is represented by the gardener.

Ceres (Demeter) goddess of the earth and protector of agriculture 'will join in the dance'. She blessed the mortals favourable to her, but punished Erysichthon, who cut down trees in a grove sacred to her, by inflicting upon him a fearful hunger that caused him to devour his own flesh (the lust of the gardener).

The gourd, the fleshy fruit used to hold liquid when dried, is very useful for Silenus who, once in the drunken state, thinks the pieces of glass from the greenhouse which were broken by Venus' arrows (love) are like pieces of gold as he places them in his wheelbarrow, the sun shining on them. Croesus was the rich king of Lydia to whom the wise Solon said, 'Count no man happy till he is dead.'

The satyrs and nymphs dance 'mazurkas' – a Polish dance in lively triple time. 'Cachucas' was a Spanish dance, and the Turks and Poles (from Cracow) have a strong folk tradition – 'stamping and trampling'.

The suggestive shape of the hay-cock resembles the suggestive dancing of the girls, whose wild movements reveal their bright undergarments, which the old gardener finds tantalizing. They play their inconsequential games among the flowers. 'Dog-skin' (fox-gloves), 'whine' and 'cower' are linked to the mad abandon of a dog playing a game.

The gardener has only his fruit to contemplate and he sees the 'fountain waves', 'thick gold honey', 'wrinkled figs', 'gourds' and 'jewels' as that Sublime Act between man and woman which is forever in his mind. He is the 'fresh evil liver' – the amorous, intoxicated, frustrated male.

That the gardens were important for the Sitwell children is evident throughout *Façade*; and the poems, taking place out of doors are full of action, interaction and communication between the characters, demonstrating that the children felt freer to indulge their fantasies when surrounded by Nature.

The Flemish gardener, Ernest de Taye, had been employed by Grandmother Sitwell at her home, 'Hay Brow', where she brought him from Ghent as a young man, on hearing of his extraordinary horticultural abilities. When she died, Sir George moved him to Renishaw, building new hot-houses and a stately gardener's cottage for him and his rotund Yorkshire wife. He was a real artist, his mind constantly preoccupied with growing and planting, and he treated the products of his labour with almost divine veneration. His strange appearance, due to the loss of all his hair, including his eyebrows, was the result of his handling a strange, exotic plant. He was always to be found working or meditating on his surroundings and was fascinated by the tall trees in the park. Osbert wrote that he watched the growth of the enormous trees, thinking of the strongest, as providers of the wood for his coffin, so that his connection with his beloved garden would remain for eternity.[1]

[1] Osbert Sitwell, *Book of Flowers* – 'In The Park' (1953).

10. A Man from a Far Countree

Rose and Alice,
Oh, the pretty lassies,
With their mouths like a calice
And their hair a golden palace –
Through my heart like a lovely wind they blow.

Though I am black and not comely,
Though I am black as the darkest trees,
I have swarms of gold that will fly like honey-bees,
By the rivers of the sun I will feed my words
Until they skip like those fleeced lambs
The waterfalls, and the rivers (horned rams),
Then for all my darkness I shall be
The peacefulness of a lovely tree –
A tree wherein the golden birds
Are singing in the darkest branches, oh!

Sunday morning. The old bell is ringing its encouragement to the surrounding countryside. Houses large and small are dotted at intervals along the narrow roads and pathways, all of which lead eventually through the centre of the shabby village to the tiny church on the hill behind.

The man is always early, standing just outside the churchyard gate. You might have thought on passing that he was waiting for someone, but in reality he is summoning the courage to follow the smart congregation, and it usually takes him until the service is about to begin before he can slip into the row at the back of the church.

His preparations on Sunday mornings are meticulous. His face and hands are scrubbed shiny, as he tries to remove all traces of the black coal-dust which has settled permanently over him during the week. There is the wrestling with the unfamiliar buttons on his suit which, though a charity handout, fits him almost perfectly, the dull brown helping to soften the ruggedness of his face.

Standing awkwardly at the back, he is free to observe the occupants of the pews in front and, as the first hymn rings out, something stirs in him as he watches the fresh young girls from the Manor singing with all their hearts.

That is why he comes to church. If there can be such beauty and joy in the world, he must one day find it. It must be so. He reassures himself as he spends his dark days in the tunnels under the ground (they call it progress), that one day he will be free. Instead of wheezing and coughing, he will stand at the front and participate, no longer a shadow that the rich and lucky walk past, unseeing.

He cannot explain it, but he feels he has found a way to gain a share. Every Sunday brings him comfort and the purpose to go on living, because he knows now that, however far off it may be, he too will one day be rewarded.

This is the only poem in *Façade* that ends on a note of optimism. Perhaps there is here a hint of Edith's religious belief, which clearly occupied her private thoughts, culminating in her acceptance in later life into the Catholic Church.

The poem uses a tree as a symbol of the social outcast, the inferior being (the black slave on the Renishaw tapestries, or the black-faced miner outside the grounds) who is filled with longing for the unattainable ('Rose and Alice'), as he stands like the tree – ugly, bare, black and gnarled in winter.

But Nature never fails. Spring will arrive. The tree with its roots embedded in the stream ('rivers of the sun') will be nurtured, receiving a new growth (the birth of the spring lambs), and the winding river, reminiscent of the ornamental writing on a scroll ('horned rams'), meanders through the country bringing new life. The blossom is followed by rich leaves tempting the chorus of birds that sing all day in its branches.

The darkness turns to gold. Hope must never be abandoned.

11. By the Lake

11. By the Lake

Across the thick and the pastel snow
Two people go ... 'And do you remember
When last we wandered this shore?' ... 'Ah no!
For it is cold-hearted December.'
'Dead, the leaves that like asses' ears hung on the trees
When last we wandered and squandered joy here;
Now Midas your husband will listen for these
Whispers – these tears for joy's bier.'
And as they walk, they seem tall pagodas;
And all the ropes let down from the cloud
Ring the hard cold bell-buds upon the trees – codas
Of overtones, ecstasies, grown for love's shroud.

Green grass.
Blue sky reflected in the clear lake.
Tiny spots of vivid colour – wild flowers.
Thick shading trees sweeping skywards.
Total happiness.
We walk to the water's edge hand in hand, brown and warm in
*   the sun.*

The scene flashes over me as we stand once more – solitary, silent.

The lake is grey, glassy.
The flat snow joins the sky without interruption. A prison of grey
*   – white cold.*
The affair is over.
Words crackle dry and empty onto the snow.
The dead cannot be brought back to life.
The tall, stark trees reach out into the grey silence – a mocking
*   reminder.*

Everyone is alone.

11. By the Lake

Edith had many difficulties to overcome in life and was constantly fighting financial, critical and personal battles. The glimmer of light in the previous poem is short-lived as we return to the real desolation of cold and painful memories. Here there is deep snow and winter – no movement: flat, still, static dead trees. (There were many dead trees. Edith's grandmother forbad them to be felled, as it made her cry.)

The leaves on the trees are long dead as winter sets in. Midas was given asses' ears by Apollo and concealed them beneath a Phrygian cap. His servant, who could not bear to keep the secret and whispered it into a hole in the ground, but the reeds grew up and revealed it: we cannot forget.

The figures resemble 'tall pagodas'. The members of Edith's family on both sides were unusually tall, and she described her aunts in this way as they walked along the sea-front. Their mode of dress and hats formed a silhouette like that of a Chinese temple.

The dead trees with branches reaching to the sky look like bell-ropes to toll the death knell: the 'coda' – concluding sounds. They are also reminiscent of the set of ropes forming part of the rigging on a sailing vessel ('shroud'), but it is 'love's shroud', 'joy's bier', the inevitable death of love after the ecstasy that dominates this waste land.

12. Country Dance

12. Country Dance

That hobnailed goblin, the bob-tailed Hob,
Said, 'It is time I began to rob'.
For strawberries bob, hob-nob with the pearls
Of cream (like the curls of the dairy girls),
And flushed with the heat and fruitish-ripe
Are the gowns of the maids who dance to the pipe.
Chase a maid?
She's afraid!
'Go gather a bob-cherry kiss from a tree,
But don't, I prithee, come bothering me!'
She said –
As she fled.
The snouted satyrs drink clouted cream
'Neath the chestnut-trees as thick as a dream;
So I went,
And leant,
Where none but the doltish coltish wind
Nuzzled my hand for what it could find.
As it neighed,
I said,
'Don't touch me, sir, don't touch me, I say,
You'll tumble my strawberries into the hay.
Those snow-mounds of silver that bee, the spring,
Has sucked his sweetness from, I will bring
With fair-haired plants and with apples chill
For the great god Pan's high altar ... I'll spill
Not one!'
So, in fun,
We rolled on the grass and began to run
Chasing that gaudy satyr the Sun;
Over the haycocks, away we ran
Crying, 'Here be berries as sunburnt as Pan!'
But Silenus
Has seen us....
He runs like the rough satyr Sun.
                    Come away!

12. Country Dance

The dairy remains cool. The heat never ceases to surprise us as we run to freedom when the work is over. Life is always light-hearted in summer.

The strawberries are rich and luscious – warmed by the sun as we bend among them, their flesh tempting and sweet. After collecting as many as our baskets will hold, we retire to our favourite vantage point at the top of the grassy hill. From there we can survey the world and, in particular, the clump of young men among the trees directly below us.

They are deep in conversation. As if we have anticipated their train of thought, we saunter towards them. If they want a game, we are ready to play.

We always pretend to be frightened (but not too much); there are so many excuses: how dare they presume!... When all else fails, we run, scattering ourselves and the bright berries in every direction. The chase continues. We are confident of winning until the inevitable fall. Even then the grass is soft and springy and we don't think of the tell-tale green stains which will have to be accounted for later.

Once caught, it is only fair to surrender the prize. But a careful watch has to be kept for the old gardener, who tends to loom alarmingly near, searching with glazed eyes.

Within seconds there is no one to be seen.

Here is the typical summer scene with the country folk enjoying themselves – harmlessly flirting – with their summer games. The setting and characters are similar to those of 'Tarantella'. Edith from her isolated position was fascinated as she observed the country children. She said she always wondered what it must be like *really* to enjoy oneself. Her contact with other children at home was limited to a few cousins and one or two select families, until her brothers were old enough to be real companions.

The rustic element is established immediately with the hobnailed boots and the mischievousness ('goblins') which affected the country lads in summer, the general rabble ('bob-tail') and drinking together ('hob-nob').

The strawberries-and-cream and ripe fruit ('fruitish-ripe')

correspond to the dairy girls who were certainly ready for their attentions (summoned to 'dance to the pipe' which Pan played).

The 'snouted satyrs' (lustful young men), were animalistic in their features and their tendencies, talking of scoring a hit (in the 'clout') with the girls, who pretend to thwart their advances ('hob' is a peg in quoits).

'Bob-cherry' (two cherries on one stem) symbolizes the breasts of the girls, which the men dream about. Later, when the girls are aroused, the 'berries as sunburnt as Pan' are their hardened nipples.

The girls know their superiority in these matters and see the boys as young horses, pleased for any encouragement: 'doltish', 'coltish', 'nuzzled', 'neighed' (dull, inexperienced and fauning). The mock displeasure at being approached and solicited changes to acquiescence in the amoral behaviour. Tempted by the apple and the pollen brought by the bees (the male ability to fertilize), they offer themselves for sacrifice ('Pan's high altar'), their breasts becoming shining objects of lust ('snow-mounds of silver'). The 'gaudy satyr the sun' is the cheap passion between the couples; the 'haycocks' again have a phallic sense; and Pan entices with his pipe, running over the hills. But Silenus (the gardener), who feels the same passion, cannot catch them because his drinking makes him unsteady on his legs and he has to be supported by the satyrs. Mortals often surround Silenus with a chain of flowers when he is drunk and asleep – the country folk at play.

13. Polka

13. Polka

' "Tra la la la la la la la
                    La!
          See me dance the polka",
Said Mr Wagg like a bear,
"With my top hat
And my whiskers that –
(Tra la la la) trap the Fair.

Where the waves seem chiming haycocks
I dance the polka; there
Stand Venus' children in their gay frocks, –
Maroon and marine, – and stare

To see me fire my pistol
Through the distance blue as my coat;
Like Wellington, Byron, the Marquis of Bristol,
Busbied great trees float.

While the wheezing hurdy-gurdy
Of the marine wind blows me
To the tune of Annie Rooney, sturdy,
Over the sheafs of the sea;

And bright as a seedsman's packet
With zinnias, candytufts chill,
Is Mrs Marigold's jacket
As she gapes at the inn door still,

Where at dawn in the box of the sailor,
Blue as the decks of the sea,
Nelson awoke, crowed like the cocks,
Then back to the dust sank he.

13. Polka

And Robinson Crusoe
Rues so
The bright and foxy beer, –
But he finds fresh isles in a negress' smiles, –
The poxy doxy dear,

As they watch me dance the polka'',
Said Mr Wagg like a bear,
"In my top hat and my whiskers that, –
Tra la la la, trap the Fair,

Tra la la la la la –
Tra la la la la la –
Tra la la la la la la la la   La   La   La!'' '

The Dandy strides towards the seafront, eagerly looking forward to what the evening must (and usually does) bring. His dress is impeccable. Feeling his normal extrovert self, now that the monotony of the day is over, he struts beside the sleepy, smart buildings lining the promenade, passes the fairground with its countless amusements and moves on into not quite so fashionable territory. Here the bars, inns and crumbling houses exude an air of squalor and neglect – in sharp contrast to the abundance of life and activity spilling over into the streets.

The women, strategically placed and conspicuous in their provocative clothing, gaze inertly as he approaches, summing him up – his gait, his manner, his finery. He is a strange intrusion into their world, appearing with predictable regularity and disappearing just as rapidly, a grotesque incompatibility which has come to be the essence of their existence.

They watch and wait. Here he is master, calls the tune, chooses his pleasure and, if only for a brief moment, can feel he is the man he would like to be.

His purpose clear, he pauses, making his customary survey. The choice is always wide, despite the occasional 'charity drives', where attempts are made by well-meaning clergy to round up and offer the women an 'honest' living at 'The Home' – a chance to

13. Polka

live a prison-like existence and work as a drudge in return for salvation … at some later date.

He wastes no time. He chooses – overpowered by the bright, tightly-fitting yellow garment hugging the thin, dark body as she stands in the doorway, welcoming him.

The night is long. The triumphal exhaustion brings with it the inevitable emptiness: the feelings of regret and guilt, and the distracted fear of the risk of disease to his otherwise fastidiously tended body.

She knows the train of thought lurking dangerously beneath the surface, and her work is not yet over. With practised ease and a smile, she restores to him his manhood.

He is Master and will return!

'Polka' means, on the one hand, a lively Bohemian dance, on the other a woman's tightly-fitting knitted jacket.

The scene is a typical seaside resort (Scarborough). The innocent enjoyment of the ordinary man, 'Mr Wagg', who needs his fun occasionally, contrasts with the more sinister side of life – the prostitute at the mercy of the male (he 'traps the fair'), or is it *she* who makes the male dance (performing 'bear')?

The Sitwell children's night nursery in Scarborough overlooked a back alley and they had an excellent view of all manner of street performers, circus folk and tramps who frequented the seaside town. Edith was also familiar with the Charity Home which her Grandmother Sitwell founded in Scarborough for the benefit and rehabilitation of Fallen Women. Here they resided and were given laundry work – or, as Edith described it, 'tore our linen to shreds once a week'.[1]

In the tight jackets, the breasts of the women look like haycocks when they dance and move mechanically like the waves of the sea. The 'Venus children' (prostitutes) attract notice by their clothes. 'Maroon' relates not only to colour, but to their trapped state in life waiting for customers and to the noise of a firework exploding ('pistol'). The pistol has a military sense with

[1] Edith Sitwell, *Taken Care Of* (1965), p. 66.

69

the blue uniforms of the Hussars ('busbied trees'), the phallic symbol implying the ultimate in dissipation ('Byron') and his activities with women. 'Wellington' also had close intimacies with various women and 'the Marquis of Bristol' (Lord Hervey), despite his clerical cloth (he was a Bishop), had little regard for his profession and morality. The Blue Hussars – a Hungarian band of Musicians spent ten days at Renishaw staying at the Sitwell Arms in the village. They provided the music for Edith's 'coming out' party, when she was 19, which had been organized on a massive scale by Sir George.

Edith often heard[1] the hurdy-gurdy playing Irish tunes ('Annie Rooney') in the street and would throw pennies down to the wandering musicians. In the poem the music entices the man to the sleazy part of town.

The clothes of the women are colourful: 'Marigold' (yellow – the name originating from the virgin), 'candytufts' (a plant with purple, pink and white tufts), 'zinnias' (colourful flowers including a deep showy red) are all intended to lure the 'seed man' (dealer in seeds) to the hotel (gaping, inviting).

The sailor in a foreign port ('blue as the decks' – blue jacket), repeats the familiar process from the beginning ('box') – the visit to the women and the male performance. 'Nelson awoke, crowed like the cocks, Then back to the dust sank he.'

The adventurer 'Crusoe' repents ('rues') his misdeeds, but the allure of the 'negress' smiles' ('doxy', beggar's wench) is too strong. ('Poxy doxy' is probably a reference to Defoe's *Roxana*.) Despite the danger of sexual disease ('poxy', with syphilis), he must have his amusement – he has not a care in the world. Tra-la-la ...

[1] Osbert Sitwell, *Left Hand Right Hand* (1945), p. 83; Sacheverell Sitwell, *An Indian Summer* (1964), p. 17.

14. Four in the Morning

Cried the navy-blue ghost
Of Mr Belaker
The allegro negro cocktail-shaker:
'Why did the cock crow,
Why am I lost
Down the endless road to Infinity toss'd?'
The tropical leaves are whispering white as water:
I race the wind in my flight down the promenade, –
Edging the far-off sand
Is the foam of the sirens' Metropole and Grand, –
As I raced through the leaves as white as water
My ghost flowed over a nursemaid, caught her,
And there I saw the long grass weep,
Where the guinea-fowl plumaged houses sleep
And the sweet ring-doves of curded milk
Watch the Infanta's gown of silk
In the ghost-room tall where the governante
Whispers slyly fading andante.
In at the window then looked he,
The navy-blue ghost of Mr Belaker,
The allegro negro cocktail-shaker, –
And his flattened face like the moon saw she, –
Rhinoceros-black yet flowing like the sea.

Not yet dawn. Still. Dark. Silent.
Strong moonlight outlines the house. Grey. Black. Silver.
Huge trees. White water. Dark-formed statues.
Curling smoke from the chimneys of the houses surrounds the
coal pits.

Peace reigns. It is the hour between sleeping and waking.

Moonlight shines through the drawing-room windows.
Empty. Shapes hint at chairs. Dark squares on the walls.
Tensions of the day dissolve in the moon's path.

14. Four in the Morning
The players have not yet entered the stage.

One turns and tosses fitfully – half-dreams – seeking solutions for the jumble of life.

Another lies still, hidden under billowing pillows, waiting for the glimmer of moonlight edged round the window to fade.

Another crunches along the sweep of the drive, past the giant statues, walking unsteadily.

It is late, the end of a long night.
The nursery curtain is cautiously pulled – the chink of moonlight widens.
The friendly ghost is seen walking across the moon's path.

Ghosts featured largely in the Sitwells' lives. Both at Renishaw and Montegufoni various ancestors were known to have been seen at intervals roaming the house or grounds, and the curious stories were always of interest to the children. It was common for Lady Ida to complain of a sleepless night and then to give as the reason that the ghosts had been about. The servants, Nurse Davis and Henry Moat in particular, knew all the details of the many legends. Although Sir George forbad such paltry pastimes as ghost stories, the children managed to satiate their appetite for these supernatural events.

In this poem Edith sees 'Mr Belaker', the ghost, as Henry Moat, her father's valet, whom she described as 'an enormous purple man, like a benevolent hippopotamus'.[1] His frequent drinking bouts gave his face the dark ('negro') blue tinge ('navy-blue' in the moonlight – also referring to the endless stories of the sea, due to his seafaring family).

The 'cocktail-shaker' implies the servant, but also a person placed above his birth and breeding (cocktail), and Henry Moat was indeed elevated to a position as companion to Sir George,

---

[1] Edith Sitwell, *Taken Care Of* (1965), p. 28.

beyond that of servant. Sir George always referred to Henry as 'the great Man', and relied on him. In Italy it was Henry who learnt the language and could communicate (he claimed that there was a similarity between Yorkshire dialect and Italian.)[1]

The poem reflects Henry's life and position in the household. 'Why did the cock crow?' – the child's cry. The servants had an intimate view of the relationship between the parents and children, and Henry often helped Edith to avoid unnecessary confrontation with her mother. His own life consisted of many adventures with women – enticed by the temptresses ('sirens'), exotic women ('tropical leaves'). His escapades occasionally led to dismissal, though he always returned before too long. (Metropole and Grand were the two hotels in Brighton where Osbert liked to stay.)

In the moonlight the leaves look white, the dew on the grass 'weeping', and the woodpigeons ('ring doves') leave an impression of watery milk ('curded milk'). The nursemaid is caught (another of Henry's conquests), and the smoke from the chimneys (grey and white in the light) resembles the 'guinea-fowl' (also grey- and white-spotted).

The 'Infanta' is Edith: the eldest daughter but not the heir. 'Governante' means ruler – Edith's mother practising her tricks on her daughter. Mr Belaker, the 'rhinoceros', with his enormous bulk surveys the silent scene. His shape is not clear through the window, but ghostly and smooth ('flattened face'). The rustle of the dress and 'whispers' are not clear-cut either, but almost unreal through the glass. The servant is the silent observer of the lives of the main characters in the household but, like a ghost, he is powerless to act. He can only watch.

On the night of Henry Moat's death, Edith relates that Osbert thought he heard someone moving about in the pantry at Renishaw, as if he had come back to look for the children he had protected so well all those years ago.[2]

---

[1] Osbert Sitwell, *The Scarlet Tree* (1946), p. 78.
[2] Edith Sitwell, *Taken Care Of* (1965), p. 28.

15. Something Lies Beyond the Scene

Something lies beyond the scene, the encre de chine, marine,
   obscene
Horizon
     In
         Hell
Black as a bison
See the tall black Aga on the sofa in the alga mope, his
Bell-rope
Moustache (clear as a great bell!)
Waves in eighteen-eighty
Bustles
Come
Late with tambourines of
Rustling
Foam.
They answer to the names
Of ancient dames and shames, and
Only call horizons their home.
Coldly wheeze (Chinese as these black-armoured fleas that dance)
   the breezes
Seeking for horizons
Wide; from her orisons
In her wide
Vermilion
Pavilion
By the seaside
The doors clang open and hide
Where the wind died
Nothing but the Princess
Cockatrice
Lean
Dancing a caprice
To the wind's tambourine.

15. Something Lies Beyond the Scene

Visitors from abroad always caused a diversion. There were presents for the children and exotic mysterious gifts for the adults, and so much to talk about! The campaigns during the distinguished years of military service, and now the well-earned life of leisure with the family.

As the talk drones on, the honoured guest becomes quieter, watching the little girl with her new toy – the gaily painted tin doll which, when wound up with the large key and set in motion, will 'dance' in jerky movements until its energy is exhausted.

'I'll call her "Princess",' she says after careful deliberation.

As he sits stiffly 'at ease' on the sofa, he can only recall his own 'princess', almost as gaudily dressed as this doll, but less incongruous against the sharp hot sand and sky.

She was his toy, waiting every afternoon casually – as if it wasn't really of consequence – outside her cool, sweet-smelling room, confident of her attractiveness and her ability to please, carrying out the wishes of her visitors. After listening to the numerous exploits recounted endlessly by his fellow officers, he felt almost tentative and hoped she wouldn't scorn his inexperience. But gradually he found his feet in this new art, and she was totally compliant, pampering his every need.

Then it suddenly changed. The orders he was supposed to give afforded little satisfaction. He did what every officer knows to avoid – fell in love with his piece of brightly-coloured tinsel! He finally admitted it to his companions and suffered on all sides during the last months. He could think only of her and lived for the short moments they spent together.

She continued to do her duty as before, and finally, as his time abroad was nearing its end, he took action. He told her. Instead of her being his slave, he wanted to reverse the roles. He loved her. What could he do?

She looked at him. Had she understood?

But a doll has no heart, shows no real emotion. Her eyes stared back – beautiful but expressionless. If he didn't come tomorrow, there would be someone else.

A toy can only perform the function for which it is made. A doll only comes to life in the mind of its owner.

15. Something Lies Beyond the Scene

The drawing-room is filled once again. The dashing officer has returned to civilian gentry life and sits confined in the stuffy drawing-room, listless and depressed. All his thoughts are of his adventures abroad – of debauchery and dissipation.

The officer's thoughts are far away across the sea ('alga', or seaweed), in that 'obscene horizon in Hell' India ('encre de chine', indian ink), or Turkey (the Aga was the commander in the Ottoman empire; an ottoman is a sofa). One was wild, and laws existed to be violated ('black as a bison', or wild ox).

The 'ancient dames and shames' – women from the oldest profession – were at the beck and call of the men; they were dependent on the men's patronage for their livelihood.

The 'black-armoured fleas' are the military men who fed off the women, as it were, like fleas. The black is due to the exposure to the sun of the Englishmen. (They are also miners, going to work, black-faced, with their picks over their shoulders at Renishaw, and 'wheezing' with lung trouble.)

The tapestries in the drawing-room with the blackboys and exotic scenes tease the memory, reminding of the 'vermilion pavilion' (oriental tent), where the men pay homage ('orisons') regardless of their reputations.

The cockatrice, or basilisk, is a serpent hatched from a cock's egg – blasting by a look (the evil eye) or its breath, throwing all caution to the wind for the sake of immediate inclinations ('caprice').

Sacheverell's tutor, Major Viburne, claimed to have come from an active military background and never hesitated to relate his braggadocio stories, although Henry Moat and the other servants had little regard for him, saying that he had never been nearer to the front line than Scarborough during the war. He had only been a member of a volunteer corps.

Wind ('wind's tambourine') features throughout *Façade*, whether as a rustle or a breeze – directionless – or as a stronger force creating waves or carrying sounds.

Street music is also important, and Edith often mentioned the playing of tambourines, mandolines, the hurdy-gurdy or barrel organ. Mechanical music performance had always interested the Sitwell children, from the days when their nurse would time

15. Something Lies Beyond the Scene

Osbert and Edith – ten minutes each – at the pianola, and they were fascinated with all forms of music boxes, which their Uncle Raincliffe collected.

16. Valse

16. Valse

'Daisy and Lily,
Lazy and silly,
Walk by the shore of the wan grassy sea, —
Talking once more 'neath a swan-bosomed tree.
Rose castles,
Tourelles,
Those bustles
Where swells
Each foam-bell of ermine,
They roam and determine
What fashions have been and what fashions will be, —
What tartan leaves born,
What crinolines worn.

By Queen Thetis,
Pelisses
Of tarlatine blue,
Like the thin plaided leaves that the castle crags grew,
Or velours d'Afrande:
On the water-gods' land
Her hair seemed gold trees on the honey-cell sand
When the thickest gold spangles, on deep water seen,
Were like twanging guitar and like cold mandoline,
And the nymphs of great caves,
With hair like gold waves,
Of Venus, wore tarlatine.
Louise and Charlottine
(Boreas' daughters)
And the nymphs of deep waters,
The nymph Taglioni, Grisi the ondine,
Wear plaided Victoria and thin Clementine
Like the crinolined waterfalls;
Wood-nymphs wear bonnets, shawls,
Elegant parasols
Floating are seen.
The Amazons wear balzarine of jonquille

16. Valse

Beside the blond lace of a deep-falling rill;
Through glades like a nun
They run from and shun
The enormous and gold-rayed rustling sun;
And the nymphs of the fountains
Descend from the mountains
Like elegant willows
On their deep barouche pillows,
In cashmere Alvandar, barège Isabelle,
Like bells of bright water from clearest wood-well.
Our élégantes favouring bonnets of blond,
The stars in their apiaries,
Sylphs in their aviaries,
Seeing them, spangle these, and the sylphs fond
From their aviaries fanned
With each long fluid hand
The manteaux espagnoles,
Mimic the waterfalls
Over the long and the light summer land.

. . .

So Daisy and Lily,
Lazy and silly,
Walk by the shore of the wan grassy sea,
Talking once more 'neath a swan-bosomed tree.
Rose castles,
Tourelles,
Those bustles!
Mourelles
Of their shade in their train follow.
Ladies, how vain, – hollow, –
Gone is the sweet swallow, –
Gone, Philomel!'

The exhibition of paintings by ―――― has been the topic of conversation in all the best drawing-rooms for weeks. Now the artistically- or socially-minded are attending the opening in order to be the first to bring up the topic at the evening's gathering. But in most cases they are hoping to be discussed in other drawing-rooms – not only as having attended but as having made such an impression that a detailed description of every item of dress will follow.

The ladies saunter past the pictures in their new spring gowns from the latest couturier – a wonderful way to show off their best day wear – spending just long enough at each frame, and exclaiming 'appropriately' or searching quickly in the catalogue for some detail to 'inspire' a thought.

But all the while, as the colourful landscape with its red poppies and cornfields, or those 'beautiful' wild flowers, are being exclaimed over and examined from every angle, the eye is actually studying – though surreptitiously – the attire of every other society lady in the room.

With practice the art is easy to perfect: simply a continual turn of the head to one's companions (real or imaginary) and a look of rapture, or puzzlement, when faced with the more 'difficult' pictures. One has a view of everyone – the striking dresses in the newest style and the softest material can all be scrutinized, the price calculated and the possibility of adaptation for one's own somewhat (in most cases) larger frame assessed in seconds.

For the artist, the gratifying numbers attending such an exhibition should not be taken too seriously as evidence of artistic appreciation; one only has to mingle with the throng of Fashionables and catch the threads of conversation to realize that the artist has so often to rely on the patronage of the wealthiest, but not necessarily the most informed, art lovers.

There is, of course, always the decision to be made, whether to buy the idyllic summer scenes – that cascading waterfall with the strange columns surrounding it, the totally incomprehensible mass of strange, harsh, but 'interesting' shapes in crude colours (one never knows ...), or the portrait of Mrs A who stands reluctantly within comparison's reach, personally explaining the finer points of the artist's inexplicable oddities.

The safest thing is to follow a well-tried 'expert' who, confident in the position as connoisseur to which her feathery companions

have elevated her, chooses a ——— and the flock follow suit; the
artist is assured a livelihood for the next decade and the afternoon
has been a success:

Another chance for the privileged to indulge in stimulating
critical conversation, the Fashion trends have been established for
the season and 'Oh Yes! – Art is Thriving!

Daisy and Lily are the perfect examples of the empty, superficial fashion-conscious sillies who walk, or rather parade, where it is essential to be seen in the latest creations. Edith held in contempt these 'faceless social climbers', as she called them,[1] and could not abide their vanity and small talk.

The poem is a detailed description of the various popular modes of attire, materials and accessories. It is set to a fast waltz rhythm (the dancing of the nymphs), but it also incorporates a broader rhythm over four bars which creates the feeling of a perpetual, even, walking rhythm which heightens the inconsequentiality of the subject matter (a certain laziness).

The materials not only refer to fashion but also represent the general preoccupation with materialism that Edith saw reflected in society.

The poem has been transposed to a natural setting. At Renishaw a favourite place of escape was the sawmill. Despite its noisy machinery, it was dominated by water cascading, swirling and falling (like fine summer materials). Edith, Osbert and Sacheverell were free to imagine that the nymphs of the forests and fountains danced and sparkled within the waters.

Daisy and Lily become not only the fashionable flappers but two flowers swaying in the sea of grasses, the rustle of the wind being their aimless chatter under the bushy trees ('swan-bosomed'). 'Foam-bells of ermine' are sweat drops in summer – it is too hot for fur. They discuss their castles ('tourelles', turrets; 'mourelles', walls) in the air ('rose castles' – rose-tinted dreams).

Throughout the poem the mythological figures and humans are all dressed in the spectrum of materials from the finest gossamer

---

[1] Edith Sitwell, *Taken Care Of* (1965), p. 158.

84

to the thickest plaid. The nymph Thetis lived in the depths of the sea, and the waterfalls were velvet, the foam at the water's edge ('honey-cell') making patterns in the sun. The 'gold spangles' look like gold threads in the water (strings from the 'mandoline') in the sunlight. The nymphs lived in the water, springs and rivers and the daughters of the north wind ('Boreas') lived in a cave. 'Ondine' (or Undine) was a water-sprite.

It was said that all persons in a state of rapture, such as poets, madmen or prophets, were caught by the water nymphs. Humans who took on the form of nymphs when they danced were the leading ballerinas 'Taglioni', who danced Sylphide in 1832, and 'Grisi', who danced Giselle in 1841. Lady Ida had been taught dancing and deportment by the famous Taglioni.

'Victoria' (stiff disapproval) and 'Clementine' (mild mercy) wear contrasting clothes (thick and thin).

At Renishaw there were two statues, the Amazon and the Warrior – guarding the entrance to the Wilderness, a part of the grounds leading to the old sawmill. Edith dressed them incongruously in muslin. The jonquil, or narcissus, implies self-worship. 'Lace' is the foam from the rivulet's 'rill', and the nun trys to avoid society's pleasures (the 'sun') by running through the open exposed ground ('glade').

There is more contrast of materials – 'cashmere', and 'barège' (gauze) – and the humans are contrasted with 'stars in their apiaries' (bees) and 'sylphs in their aviaries' (birds). The sylph is both a nymph and a type of humming-bird with a long tail ('long fluid hand'). In lace mantillas ('bonnets of blond') and 'manteaux espagnoles' (Spanish capes moving like sheets of water – 'mimic the waterfalls'), 'Daisy' and 'Lily' build their castles in the air.

The swallow and the nightingale ('Philomel') have migrated. Summer is over.

17. Jodelling Song

'We bear velvet cream.
Green and babyish
Small leaves seem; each stream
Horses' tails that swish,

And the chimes remind
Us of sweet birds singing,
Like the jangling bells
On rose trees ringing.

Man must say farewells
To parents now,
And to William Tell
And Mrs. Cow.

Man must say farewells
To storks and Bettes,
And to roses' bells,
And statuettes.

Forests white and black
In spring are blue
With forget-me-nots,
And to lovers true

Still the sweet bird begs
And tries to cozen
Them: "Buy angels' eggs
Sold by the dozen."

Gone are clouds like inns
On the gardens' brinks,
And the mountain djinns,–
Ganymede sells drinks;

While the days seem grey,
And his heart of ice,
Grey as chamois, or
The edelweiss,

And the mountain streams
Like cowbells sound–
Tirra lirra, drowned
In the waiter's dreams

Who has gone beyond
The forest waves,
While his true and fond
Ones seek their graves.'

The first job. The longed for, yet fearful, chance to taste the real world away from the tiny mountain village. True, he is not far from home – if one could fly – but it seems at least a world away below the clouds.

Grey: grey stone, grey streets, grey-faced people hurrying about their business. He longs for the strong sun, the crisp dry air – the Alpine Silence which intensifies every tiny sound – running water, birds and insects – with the occasional cowbell as its wearer lumbers across the grasses in complete contentment.

Solitude – but he is not alone. He belongs to the mountain. He would never understand the world below.

The café is brimming with steamy people seeking a short respite from the grey outside. The traditional 'Zvieri pause', or coffee hour, is an essential part of any day. The elderly can enjoy the rich cream cakes, achieving a purpose for each day which they otherwise lack now that society has no more use for them; the numerous mothers with small children seeking an escape from the endless domesticity which will be their lot for years to come, and the small children themselves, seeking to demand the largest, stickiest piece of Blackforest cake, which they will proceed to smear over themselves, the chairs, the tables and anyone else who comes within reach of their chocolate- and cream-laden fingers.

17. Jodelling Song

*As if in a dream, the Alp boy negotiates the tables in his neat,
white jacket, writing stiffly and slowly the orders for hot
chocolate or coffee, and wheeling the cream-laden trolley before
him, tempting each customer who is faced with the devastating
task of choosing some rich, sweet sustenance.*

*Food may be a great comforter in some circumstances, but he
can only think of his old goatherd, and the occasional colours of
wild flowers among the bare rocks; and he feels cheated that life's
alternative to the cosy family is to descend from the heights of the
mountains to the friendless depths of despair.*

If this is growing up, he wishes to remain a child forever.

This poem was inspired by Gertrude Stein's 'Accents in Alsace',
but Edith has set it in German-speaking Switzerland. She recalls
spring with its delicate leaves, water gushing down the mountains
as the snow melts, cows wearing the typical bells, and William
Tell (the Robin Hood of Switzerland).

The stork is also a familiar sight, symbolizing the strong
relationship between parents and young; beds ('Bettes') are other
very personal familiar objects.

The 'statuettes' are the bare rock formations, or peaks, small in
the distance. The Alps have a tempting quality which can prove
treacherous. They seem so beautiful, but within minutes a
complete weather change takes place. One can be cheated so
easily ('cozen'). The mountains are full of contrast: from the
forget-me-nots in spring to the dark forests of winter.

Death is imminent ('gardens' brinks') and one is already half-
human, half-angel ('djinns' were the spirits in Mohammedan
demonology). Ganymede, the waiter, was carried off to fill the
cup of Zeus and live among the gods on Mount Olympus.

Chamois are the wild goats; edelweiss is the white flower that
grows among rocks.

'Beyond the forest waves' refers to the Alpine tree-line where,
at a certain altitude, the trees give way to bare rock. One has
either gone up to eternal rest or down under the earth.

Edith, who hated travelling, sums up Switzerland (life), famous
for its alps (beauty), its tourist attractions and cafés (indulgence).
The essence for the traveller is its transience.

18. Scotch Rhapsody

18. Scotch Rhapsody

'Do not take a bath in Jordan,
                                        Gordon,
On the holy Sabbath, on the peaceful day!'
Said the huntsman, playing on his old bagpipe,
Boring to death the pheasant and the snipe—
Boring the ptarmigan and grouse for fun—
Boring them worse than a nine-bore gun.
Till the flaxen leaves where the prunes are ripe,
Heard the tartan wind a-droning through the pipe,
And they heard Macpherson say:
'Where do the waves go? What hotels
Hide their bustles and their gay ombrelles?
And would there be room? – Would there be *room*? *Would* there
    be room for me?'
There is a hotel at Ostend
Cold as the wind, without an end,
Haunted by ghostly poor relations
Of Bostonian conversations
(Like bagpipes rotting through the walls.)
And there the pearl-ropes fall like shawls
With a noise like marine waterfalls.
    And 'Another little drink wouldn't do us any harm'
Pierces through the sabbatical calm.
And that is the place for me!
So do not take a bath in Jordan, Gordon,
On the holy Sabbath on the peaceful day—
Or you'll never go to heaven, Gordon Macpherson,
And speaking purely as a private person
That is the place—*that* is the place— that is the *place* for me!

*To the casual guest the dim room appears strange, with its odd
collection of walking-sticks propped against the low tables, which
in turn hold an array of monocles, ear-trumpets, yellowing
newspapers and dusty water-glasses presided over by brown-
filled decanters. Within the deep chairs the small, skeletal,*

91

18. Scotch Rhapsody

wizened figures wait, poised ready for the repetition of yet another day in the boarding-house.

All have seen better times. The women, tattered and faded, reflect the worn-out draperies and threadbare furniture surrounding them. The men, grotesquely gnarled, abuse the signs of their physical decline and attempt to maintain the last vestiges of comradeship by means of the continuous tipple. This has become the only respite from the relentless process of degeneration, as each seeks his own way of breaking through the crippling isolation which old age and infirmity have brought.

The initial silence gradually builds up to a restless activity; occasional mutterings, murmurings and rustlings, with here and there a flash of coherence – the old hunting stories, memories of travel abroad, plans for the future – repeated loudly and at regular intervals for any who care to listen and, perhaps, comprehend?

The sedentary monotony is broken quite frequently (depending upon the degree of liquid consumption) and the slow struggle begins: to leave the drawing-room, cross the dark hallway and reach the 'sanctuary' with its damp and antiquated plumbing of dubious reliability, in keeping with the vulnerable state of its habitual occupants.

The unvarying days allow plenty of time to re-live the past, but there is no way back to youth and health, just as there is no way any longer to control the future. The rapidly nearing finale, the total disintegration which dominates the powerless body, is bearable only to those who desperately believe there is another world to move on to; and, if that be the case, they have obeyed the rules of life and can be confident of the reward.

Edith as a child had ample opportunity to observe the older generation, and she often commented on the incredible age of the servants whom Grandmother Londesborough employed, such as Leckly, the 'incredibly ancient' lady's maid.[1] Edith also stayed in a boarding-house near Lancaster Gate to have her tonsils out, and she recounts how the guests were all extremely old and in a state of decay and disrepair, just waiting to expire.[2]

[1] Edith Sitwell, *Taken Care Of* (1965), p. 60.
[2] Ibid., p. 53.

18. Scotch Rhapsody

The name 'Scotch Rhapsody' is very appropriate; 'scotched' is to be maimed or disabled (but not yet dead), and 'rhapsody' implies irregularity, emotional and otherwise. Macpherson was Grandmother Londesborough's chief gardener. The river Jordan, with its youthful waters, gives re-birth; but there is no point at this late stage in life. A 'Jordan' is also a chamber pot.

The huntsman playing the 'bag-pipe' (windbag), repeats endlessly the old hunting stories so boring ('nine-bore gun') as senility sets in (the leaves are 'flaxen', withering), but allusion is also made to the malfunction of the digestive tracts of the old (with 'wind', 'prunes', 'pipes'), and the difficulties are not only physical. The attempt to grasp the future is uppermost in the mind. Where does one go? Is there life after death? The malfunctioning mind, due to old age, wonders if it will be like that distantly recalled 'hotel at Ostend' over the sea, now ghostly 'old' and 'rotting'.

The 'pearl-ropes' break – the most prized possessions and achievements are no longer important. As one looks at the withered bodies (the 'shawls' fall off the shoulders, the flesh is almost gone). The 'marine waterfalls' and 'bagpipes rotting' signify the breakdown of the intricate system in the old bodies and the plumbing in the old rooms.

Drink is in the end no consolation. One must prepare for afterwards ('heaven') if one wants to be sure of a place.

19. Popular Song
For Constant Lambert

Lily O'Grady,
Silly and shady,
Longing to be
A lazy lady,
Walked by the cupolas, gables in the
Lake's Georgian stables,
In a fairy tale like the heat intense,
And the mist in the woods when across the fence
The children gathering strawberries
Are changed by the heat into negresses,
Though their fair hair
Shines there
Like gold-haired planets, Calliope, Io,
Pomona, Antiope, Echo, and Clio.
Then Lily O'Grady,
Silly and shady,
Sauntered along like a
Lazy lady;
Beside the waves' haycocks her gown with tucks
Was of satin the colour of shining green ducks,
And her fol-de-rol
Parasol
Was a great gold sun o'er the haycocks shining,
But she was a negress black as the shade
That time on the brightest lady laid.
Then a satyr, dog-haired as trunks of trees,
Began to flatter, began to tease,
And she ran like the nymphs with golden foot
That trampled the strawberry, buttercup root,
In the thick gold dew as bright as the mesh
Of dead Panope's golden flesh,
Made from the music whence were born
Memphis and Thebes in the first hot morn,
–And ran, to wake
In the lake,
Where the water-ripples seem hay to rake.

19. Popular Song

And Charlottine,
Adeline,
Round rose-bubbling Victorine,
And the other fish
Express a wish
For mastic mantles and gowns with a swish;
And bright and slight as the posies
Of buttercups and of roses,
And buds of the wild wood-lilies
They chase her, as frisky as fillies.
The red retriever-haired satyr
Can whine and tease her and flatter,
But Lily O'Grady,
Silly and shady,
In the deep shade is a lazy lady;
Now Pompey's dead, Homer's read,
Heliogabalus lost his head,
And shade is on the brightest wing,
And dust forbids the bird to sing.

You can see her every day – walking along the path which separates the private grounds from the public terrain. For those who do not know the story, she has an air and carriage that foretell a woman of importance and breeding, and many a stranger has enquired along the road as to the identity of the richly clad lady. She always walks with her beautiful gold sunshade spread wide, shielding her face from the heat of the sun, and one imagines the lily-white, neat features and the slim hands supporting the parasol.

She stops to watch the children play – they are bronzed by the long summer sun – and they laugh and sing while they hunt for wild fruit. At first they were slightly in awe, even frightened, because she talked so strangely, and they weren't sure if her words were meant for them; but now they ignore her presence and she continues to stare at them and mutter.

The fun starts when the young folk from the farm spot her. In their high spirits, they tease and wheedle and beg, imitating her strange accent until, on being forced to acknowledge their existence, she turns and heads quickly for the village. But they won't leave her alone, taunting and questioning her until her ducal manner has worn away. Then, looking wild and with a few choice words, she snaps her parasol shut and reveals her face, much the worse for wear and painted as if she has used a cracked and jagged mirror. The clothes are handsome, but is the price too high?

Lily O'Grady, the miner's daughter, has paid with her self-respect for her pleasure, the finery and flattery.

The delusion of grandeur can't last; her hey-day is over.

The summer is near its end, the colours tired and the leaves wilting. Her aspirations have been too high. The downfall has to come, and now only her parasol can conceal what time has done.

But she will never know – she will not follow her body, but her mind, which lives on in the world she desires and briefly achieves.

The scene for this poem is the same as for 'Country Dance', with the nymphs and satyrs (country folk) taunting and soliciting favours from Lily O'Grady, the Irish girl no longer so young and of dubious honesty ('shady'). She dreams of a privileged life with luxurious surroundings ('Georgian' elegance).

She can no longer accept the reality ('fairy tale'), as her cheapened life has not made her any happier. She envies the innocence of the children, who represent the Muses, the goddesses of song (with their hair gold from the sun, they seemed heavenly bodies).

Calliope was the Muse of epic poetry, Clio the Muse of history. Pomona was the divinity of fruits (the green-yellow colour was Edith's favourite). Antiope was the mother, by Jupiter, of Amphion, who marched against Thebes. Echo, a mountain nymph, talked incessantly to Hera, to distract her from Zeus's amours, until she finally pined away. Io, seduced by Zeus, was turned by Hera into a cow, and a gad-fly drove her into a state of frenzy until she rested on the banks of the Nile. Lily O'Grady was also to be compared to the frenzied state.

The 'fol-de-rol' (the role of an actor, or pretence), acted to hide

19. Popular Song

her true self, like the 'parasol', which seems like the sun. The 'satyr dog-haired' (fond of sensual pleasure and drink – 'whine' is a pun on wine), knows he will succeed with her, like the 'retriever'. She is destroyed and too old ('Memphis' and 'Thebes', important cities until they fell) and her rubbery skin ('mastic mantle') has succumbed to the effects of indolence and sloth. She is no longer agile like a sea-nymph ('Panope'). Her reign is over – 'Pompey's dead'. 'Homer's read' – she can no longer learn. Heliogabalus, the Roman Emperor, was made priest of the sun god and was a prince of the most incredible folly, vice and superstition.

This outdoor poem is full of activity and interaction, which is an effect of the warmth in summer and the countryside. Osbert described the two contrasting populations inhabiting the surrounds of Renishaw: the rustic, white and stationary population labouring by day in the open countryside and the shifting masses of black miners who worked day and night under the earth.

20. Fox-Trot 'Old Sir Faulk'

                    Old
                        Sir
                            Faulk,
        Tall as a stork,
Before the honeyed fruits of dawn were ripe, would walk,
And stalk with a gun
The reynard-coloured sun,
Among the pheasant-feathered corn the unicorn has torn, forlorn
    the
Smock-faced sheep
Sit
    And
        Sleep;
Periwigged as William and Mary, weep ...
'Sally, Mary, Mattie, what's the matter, why cry?'
The huntsman and the reynard-coloured sun and I sigh;
'Oh, the nursery-maid Meg
With a leg like a peg
Chased the feathered dreams like hens, and when they laid an egg
In the sheepskin
Meadows
Where
The serene King James would steer
Horse and hounds, then he
From the shade of a tree
Picked it up as spoil to boil for nursery tea,' said the mourners.
    In the
Corn, towers strain,
Feathered tall as a crane,
And whistling down the feathered rain, old Noah goes again—
An old dull mome
With a head like a pome,
Seeing the world as a bare egg,
Laid by the feathered air; Meg
Would beg three of these
For the nursery teas

20. Fox-Trot 'Old Sir Faulk'

Of Japhet, Shem, and Ham; she gave it
Underneath the trees,
Where the boiling
       Water
        Hissed,
Like the goose-king's feathered daughter–kissed,
Pot and pan and copper kettle
Put upon their proper mettle,
Lest the Flood – the Flood – the Flood begin again through these!

The wild hunter puts on his new grass-green hunting suit, picks up his hunting pouch, powder-horn and gun, and walks quickly to the fields.

He wears glasses and wants to kill the hare.

The hare sits hidden among the leaves and makes fun of the hunter behind his back.

After a while the sun shines fiercely and his gun feels heavy, so he lies down on the green grass.

The hare watches it all, and when the hunter is sleeping and begins to snore, the hare steals up to him and takes his gun and his glasses without a sound and creeps stealthily away.

The hare puts the glasses on and decides he would like to shoot with the gun.

The hunter is terrified and runs away, shouting 'Help, somebody, Help!'

At last the wild hunter comes to a deep well. He jumps in head first. There is not a moment to lose.

The hare fires the gun.

The hunter's wife sits at the window drinking from her coffee-cup. The hare shoots her in two.

'Oh no! Oh no!' screams the woman.

The hare's son, baby hare, sits hidden in the green grass.

The coffee pours on to his nose, and he cries out: 'Who has burnt me?' And he waves the coffee spoon in his hand.

20. Fox-Trot 'Old Sir Faulk'

The title 'Foxtrot' (an American dance), relates already to hunting. Old Sir Faulk was the father of two little girls, Mollie and Gladys Hume, who were Edith's only friends when she was four or five, apart from her cousin Veronica. Colonel Hume reminded Edith of a character in the German children's book of cautionary tales *Struwwelpeter*: he was tall and, as she recalled, stork-like. She imagined him stalking his prey with his gun – the terrified hare fleeing before him. However, she transposed the countryside round the poem to Radburne, where another family friend and neighbour, Colonel Chandos-Pole, lived.

Edith said that *Struwwelpeter* was a great influence on her poetry.[1] While Sir Faulk is away hunting, stalking through the ears of corn, the ritual and formality of the nursery tea has been disturbed (as if a unicorn had attacked with its horn), and the children in fresh chemises cluster timidly together, crying 'smock-faced sheep'. This incident in the poem refers to the visit Edith paid the family just after their mother had died, and she could not understand why they should cry. To her it would have been no reason to cry!

Anyway, it was not correct to cry at tea – the children must behave. To distract them, their nurse read from the Bible ('King James') which was enough to spoil their tea. Japhet, Shem and Ham represent the children crying again ('feathered rain' the tears, the 'feathered dreams' their mother). Momus (the god of censure, 'old dull mome') would correct them for their manners and misdemeanours.

The story of Noah's flood shows the punishment for the wicked world – this is also the message behind the *Struwwelpeter* stories. The kettle boiling (more water – tears) and put on 'its proper mettle' (the usual lecture to be good) results only in more 'floods' of tears.

The ultimate in repression.

[1] Edith Sitwell, *Taken Care Of* (1965), p. 33.

21. Sir Beelzebub

21. Sir Beelzebub

When
Sir
Beelzebub called for his syllabub in the hotel in Hell
     Where Proserpine first fell,
Blue as the gendarmerie were the waves of the sea,
     (Rocking and shocking the bar-maid).
Nobody comes to give him his rum but the
Rim of the sky hippopotamus-glum
Enhances the chances to bless with a benison
Alfred Lord Tennyson crossing the bar laid
With cold vegetation from pale deputations
Of temperance workers (all signed In Memoriam)
Hoping with glory to trip up the Laureate's feet,
     (Moving in classical metres) ...
Like Balaclava, the lava came down from the
Roof, and the sea's blue wooden gendarmerie
Took them in charge while Beelzebub roared for his rum.
     ... None of them come!

They found him lying on the pier. Three or four layers of tattered coats, shiny with oily sweat and grime and two leathery shapes for shoes with gaping holes, revealing blue-and-black flesh: in one hand, a half-empty bottle of whisky and in the other a paper bag filled with smithereens of glass, obviously created with violence but now tinkling pathetically as they attempt to move him.

But it is the head that causes the officers to stare in bizarre fascination: the huge mass of dark blue and purple colour from months of dirt; the unkempt wild hair spread on the ground, eyes staring upwards, mouth open.

Has his departure from earth come as a surprise? Or is it a prophetic utterance for the benefit of the world he has left behind? Between the long grey planks the foaming water can be seen moving restlessly, but the sound of the waves breaking on the shore, so complacent in their regularity, foretells the future — Life remains unchanged.

21. Sir Beelzebub

The circle is complete. The façade is penetrated. The real moral values so discreetly hidden in the drawing-room in 'Hornpipe' are now exposed.

The Devil – Sir Beelzebub – has done his work: this poem shows the total disintegration of man through his own folly – drink. He is now the total outcast from society ('Proserpine first fell': Proserpine was the daughter of Ceres, the wife of Hades and queen of the shades).

From his cell in gaol – Hell (the cell implies a barrier of bars, the long steel grass) – he can only call drunkenly for more liquid. The frothy 'syllabub' – a traditional recipe, a mixture of brandy and dairy cream – links the dairy maids (now barmaids) with the outdoor poems.

The police are in 'blue' uniforms (like the 'waves of the sea'). The uniform is also a sign of privilege (military life) and a reason for indulgence.

The rocking movement is like the waves or the rocking-horse, but is due to unsteadiness through intoxication (Silenus). Sir Bacchus, the lover of wine and fast-living in 'Hornpipe', is now transformed into Sir Beelzebub (the Devil).

He is alone in his cell – without visitors, abandoned, unloved. The 'rim of the sky' is the skylight, or cell window, which shows only grey sky ('hippopotamus glum'), emphasizing the hopelessness of his situation.

Perhaps he will repent. His chance comes when the prison do-gooders visit – reformists ('temperance workers') preaching salvation, giving a blessing ('benison') and leaving suitable reading material ('Crossing the Bar') in the cell ('cold vegetation') to help him mend his ways. But really they are only wanting the laurels for good works themselves. The selfishness shines through the charity.

This is his final chance to redeem himself (reading Tennyson, as Queen Victoria did in 'Hornpipe'). But he does not listen, the 'Balaclava' (helmet) covers his ears (the Balaclava light brigade lined the nave at Tennyson's funeral) and he is doomed – 'Into the mouth of Hell rode the six hundred.' He destroyed his world. It has fallen about his ears and he will end up in hell covered with burning earth ('lava').

21. Sir Beelzebub

He will not change his ways and will die as he lived!

Edith was very sensitive to all manner of tramps and those less fortunate than herself. To the chagrin of her father, she could never resist giving whatever money she had to anyone who she felt needed it. She often cried at the plight of many of her fellow human beings.

A child runs barefoot along the sands. Her feet enjoy the cool foam washing over them. She skips under the shadow of the pier and out into the early morning sun. She splashes along the thin line where land and sea become one.